The Secrets Of Dark Psychology and Body Language

How to Protect Yourself From Manipulation, Detect Lies, and Analyze Other People. 7 Rules of Influence and Power.

RONALD GILL

© **Copyright 2023 - All rights reserved.**

The content inside this book may not be duplicated, reproduced, or transmitted without direct written permission from the author or publisher.

Under no circumstances will any blame or legal responsibility be held against the publisher, or author, for any damages, reparation, or monetary loss due to the information contained within this book, either directly or indirectly.

Legal Notice:

This book is copyright protected. It is only for personal use. You cannot amend, distribute, sell, use, quote or paraphrase any part, or the content within this book, without the consent of the author or publisher.

Disclaimer Notice:

Please note the information contained within this document is for educational and entertainment purposes only. All effort has been executed to present accurate, reliable, up to date, complete information. No warranties of any kind are declared or implied. Readers acknowledge that the author is not engaging in the rendering of legal, financial, medical, or professional advice. The content within this book has been derived from various sources. Please consult a licensed professional before attempting any techniques outlined in this book.

By reading this document, the reader agrees that under no circumstances is the author responsible for any losses, direct or indirect, that are incurred as a result of the use of the information contained within this document, including, but not limited to, errors, omissions, or inaccuracies.

TABLE OF CONTENT

INTRODUCTION	4
CHAPTER 1: Why You Need to Know The Secrets of Dark Psychology	7
CHAPTER 2: The Dark Triad	11
CHAPTER 3: Narcissism	20
CHAPTER 4: Machiavellianism	37
CHAPTER 5: Psychopathy	46
CHAPTER 6: Manipulation	54
CHAPTER 7: Deception	65
CHAPTER 8: Gaslighting	75
CHAPTER 9: Love-Bombing	84
CHAPTER 10: Is Someone Using You?	95
CHAPTER 11: Decoding Body Language Clues	102
CHAPTER 12: How to Protect Yourself	110
CHAPTER 13: 7 Rules of Influence and Power	123
CONCLUSION	128

INTRODUCTION

In this modern world where you're more susceptible to psychological exploitation and covert manipulation than ever, it has become imperative to fortify yourself with the tools and knowledge needed to safeguard yourself.

The Secrets of Dark Psychology and Body Language serve as a guide to help you navigate the vicious terrain of dark psychology and equip you with strategies to protect yourself. Within this book, you and I will embark on a journey of exploration.

Together, we will uncover the secrets of dark psychology and the tactics employed by dark psychology practitioners, including psychological manipulation, deception, gaslighting, narcissistic abuse, and more.

On this journey, we will employ a powerful tool you didn't know you have in your arsenal: body language analysis. The human body is a labyrinth of expressions and learning to decode its subtle cues can provide valuable insight into the true emotional states and intentions of others.

We will deep-dive into the ocean of nonverbal communication, unraveling the nuances of body movements, gestures, facial expressions, and other body language clues. By mastering the art of analyzing body language, you can establish an extra layer of protection against manipulative forces.

Beyond this, we will also discuss the importance of building self-awareness, establishing personal boundaries, and developing assertiveness skills. Armed with these three skills, you can navigate the murky waters of interpersonal interactions with confidence and clarity.

It is my sincere hope that this book will empower you to fortify your mind, protect your mental and emotional well-being, and build authentic connections rooted in trust and a healthy bond. Together, let's begin this journey of transformation. In the end, I trust you will emerge stronger, wiser, and unrelenting in the face of dark psychology and manipulation.

Want to Master 7 Proven Ways to Strengthen Your Mind?

SCAN THE QR CODE NOW

CHAPTER 1:
Why You Need to Know The Secrets of Dark Psychology

"Maybe we all have darkness inside of us and some of us are better at dealing with it than others."

– Jasmine Warga.

Everyone has a dark side, which we try to suppress, control, and hide from others. Your unique relationship with your dark side can define who you become. And dark psychology is how we understand people's relationship with their dark sides. When people talk about dark psychology, they say it is a field of study, a science, or an art – it is none of these.

Most people know that psychology is defined as the study of human behavior. However, fewer people are familiar with the concept of dark psychology and what it entails. Yet, it continues to fascinate millions of people.

Individuals who are interested in dark psychology fall into two categories. The first are those who want to learn as much as possible about dark psychology to protect themselves from its tricks and strategies.

Meanwhile, the second category is those who research dark psychology to know how to use its tools and devices to get what they want.

If dark psychology isn't a field of study or branch of psychology, what is it?

At its core, the phenomenon called dark psychology exploits the weaknesses of the human mind. Dark psychology enthusiasts work hard to understand how humans think, feel, and behave to manipulate or influence them to do whatever they want – whether it's buying a product or staying in an abusive relationship.

It is primarily about the application of mind control and manipulation tactics. Where psychology focuses on human thoughts, emotions, and behaviors, dark psychology focuses on techniques, strategies, and tactics of manipulation, coercion, motivation, and persuasion.

These strategies can empower an individual to subtly control another person without the victim's awareness or consent. It is beneficial for the person using it in mild cases, however in severe cases, it can inflict harm on the victim or steal their independence.

I think of dark psychology as both a consciousness construct and the nature of humans to prey on each other. Selfish, criminal, narcissistic, or psychopathic intentions may drive someone to use manipulation and other tactics.

Unlike the rest of humanity, dark psychology practitioners prey on people's weaknesses and vulnerabilities to subtly change their behavior or perception of others using underhanded means. We all have a dark side; therefore, we can all exploit others' weaknesses to our advantage. Yet, most human beings control the impulses to act on this dark side.

"Is dark psychology even real?"

This is one question I often encounter from people who are interested in protecting themselves from this evil practice. And my answer is always, "Yes, it is very real – as real as the blue sky or the hair on our heads."

Although we may not always call it dark psychology, psychological manipulation is a fact today. We've all experienced it, whether we know it or not. Anyone familiar with dark psychologists and their power games knows how real it is.

But if you're reading this right now, that's an indication that you

aren't attuned to dark psychologists. The good news is you're in the right place because we will look at examples of how dark psychology is applied in everyday interactions.

Nobody wants to be a victim of manipulation, but chances are it has already happened to you at least once in your lifetime. And if we're being realistic, it has most likely happened multiple times without your awareness.

You may not have met a dark psychology user, but every day, people like you and I are exposed to shady tactics and strategies daily. After all, they are employed in ads, social media posts, sales techniques, and even your supervisor's behavior.

Suppose you're a parent. The people you trust the most tend to use these covert manipulation and dark persuasion strategies on you. In that case, even your kids will try to use the tactics on you as they experiment with different behaviors to achieve autonomy and get what they want.

Examples of dark psychology can be seen in nearly all aspects of life. While it's arguably dominant in romantic or interpersonal relationships, you will find its use in different parts of life. For example, a coworker might start a power play at work to try to one-up you.

The purpose of this chapter isn't to tell you how to protect yourself from manipulation and exploitation. We will do that in a subsequent chapter as we delve deeper into the rabbit hole that is dark psychology.

I want you to know that it's easy to fall victim to these tactics. You may be using them on others without knowing you're doing something wrong and unethical. So, let me challenge you to assess different areas of your life, from work to parenting, friendships, romantic relationships, and leadership. You might be shocked to find that you're employing these unsavory practices in your everyday interactions with the people in your life.

While some are deliberate about taking advantage of others using dark psychology tactics, many use them unknowingly because they picked it up in childhood – most likely from parents or other adults with authority over them as a child. Others learned it by happenstance.

For example, they may have tried to manipulate someone unintentionally, found out it got them what they wanted, and stuck to it ever since.

Just as there are books and courses teaching people how to protect themselves from dark psychology, thousands of courses and programs are aimed at those who want to know how to use it to get what they want. So, you have those who train to learn these tactics. And these are people you will meet either online or in real life.

So, you can see why ordinary, everyday people like you must know as much as they can about the secrets of dark psychology.

If you're familiar with how these tactics work, you will be able to protect and defend yourself against them. Additionally, if you ever find yourself in a situation requiring you to employ dark psychology techniques, you can be sure you're using them correctly and ethically. The bottom line is that we can all benefit from knowing more about the darker side of human psychology.

In the next chapter, you will learn in-depth about the dark triad personality and how to watch out for them.

CHAPTER 2:
The Dark Triad

Morally, ethically, and socially questionable behavior is a fact of life, and there are instances of selfish, ruthless, unscrupulous, and sometimes downright evil behavior in every culture and across history.

You've met some people who are challenging to deal with. They are usually arrogant, overbearing, and volatile. Interactions with them can be draining. Yet, you can carefully manage a relationship with them if you set some boundaries.

However, there is a group of people with behaviors and traits that are highly damaging to everyone around them. These traits are toxic and can destroy those that get into a relationship with those who have them. Psychology calls them the "Dark Triad" traits.

If you're familiar with psychology, you've likely heard about the Dark Triad, as the phrase is a buzzword in this field. But if you aren't, you might think I'm talking about a horror movie or TV show when, in fact, it's what psychology calls a disturbing cocktail of harmful personality traits.

The umbrella term for personality types linked to antagonistic behavior classes is "dark traits." The Dark Triad is the most prominent of these dark traits.

The term "Dark Triad" was coined in 2002 by psychology researchers Delroy L. Paulhus and Kevin M. Williams and was first published in the Journal of Research and Personality. It refers to a mix of three distinct but interconnected harmful personality types. You're probably familiar with the traits themselves:

- Narcissism

- Machiavellianism
- Psychopathy

A dark triad personality will say or do anything to get their way – usually at the expense of others. They tend to be manipulative, callous, and devoid of empathy. Individuals with any of these dark triad personality types are particularly more evil than the average person.

They have an inflated self-perception and will shamelessly promote themselves to whoever they deem powerful or influential. These people are predisposed to impulsive and dangerous behavior – committing crimes in some cases – with zero regards for the impact of their actions on others.

While many researchers believe Narcissism, Machiavellianism, and Psychopathy are different traits with overlapping features, others argue that there is an underlying construct research has yet to unravel fully. They call this the "D – Dark Factor of personality."

D is "the general tendency to maximize one's utility – disregarding, accepting, or provoking disutility for other people – accompanied by beliefs that serve as justification."

D describes a person's tendency to ruthlessly pursue their interests or goals even at the expense of others (and, in some cases, to harm others) while having a belief system that justifies their actions and behaviors.

In the above definition, utility is used to mean goal achievement. People with a high D-factor seek to maximize their goal achievement, i.e., accomplish their goals, even when it contrasts with the interests of others or creates a negative outcome for others.

Note that goal achievement in this context does not refer to things that do not affect others, such as having consensual sex or engaging in leisure activities. Another thing to note is that those who have a high "D" are rarely uncooperative with others. Instead, they strategically choose when or who to cooperate with.

Important to note is that the dark triad can engage in self-motivated activities that benefit others. Still, the critical disposition is their willingness to endure high personal costs to make another person suffer a more substantial cost.

Just as important to note is the presence of beliefs that justify their malicious behaviors, such as a belief that they're superior to others, cynicism, rejection of universal moral codes, and an endorsement of ideologies that promote individual or group dominance.

"D" is a fundamental, general dispositional inclination, meaning that it's the underlying reason behind any aversive trait or malevolent behavior (such as cheating, bullying, intimidating, exploiting, hurting, harassing, stealing, trolling, abusing, manipulating, etc.).

Utility in goal achievement includes various visible gains, including money, thrill, pleasure, joy, status, and fulfillment. Thus, individuals with a high D-factor will derive goal achievement (for example, fun) from the disutility others suffer (for example, pain).

Based on research, the nine dark traits marked by the D-factor are:

1. **Egoism** – An excessive preoccupation with one's advantage or pleasure at the expense of individual or communal well-being.
2. **Moral disengagement** – A cognitive orientation to society that differentiates a person's thinking in a way that promotes unethical behavior.
3. **Machiavellianism** – An orientation of manipulativeness, strategic calculation, and callous affect.
4. **Psychological entitlement** – A stable, perversive sense that one is more deserving and entitled than others.

5. **Self-interest** – The pursuit of achievements in socially valued areas, such as social status, recognition, material gains, recognition, career, or academic accomplishment.
6. **Spitefulness** – A preference to cause financial, physical, or social harm to another, which also entails harming oneself.
7. **Narcissism** – A preoccupation with ego reinforcement.
8. **Sadism** – An affinity for inflicting deliberate physical, psychological, or sexual pain on others for pleasure or to assert power and dominance.
9. **Psychopathy** – Deficits in callousness, affect, impulsivity, and self-control.

Here's a summary of key findings from psychology researchers on the nine dark traits:

- All dark traits are positively interrelated – although some, such as the dark triad, relate more strongly with each other than the rest.
- The traits most strongly connected to "D" are linked in aspects of the theoretical model: utility maximization (I'll get whatever I want in any way possible," causing disutility to others (I don't mind suffering minor harm to punish someone who deserves it), and justifying beliefs (I am more deserving than others).
- Those who score high on "D" are more likely to behave unethically or keep material gains for themselves in the face of an opportunity.
- "D" relates to many potential outcomes, such as positive associations with dominance, power, aggression, insensitivity, impulsivity, and negative associations with empathy, modesty, perspective taking, fairness, greed avoidance, internalized moral identity, sincerity, and nurturance.

The dark triad traits exist on a continuum. Individuals with this toxic mix of personality traits mask their intentions with a charming and charismatic disposition. They can undermine the people in their lives and leave a lasting negative impact.

People with these traits are ready to exploit anyone, from coworkers to closest family, to get ahead in life, and they rarely experience remorse when they inflict harm or suffering on others. They are also incredibly aggressive and duplicitous.

You might wonder how these individuals can conceal their true nature. Is it possible to hide such darkness from others? How can you know people with actual dark triad traits?

Many behavioral and physical cues are associated with the three traits. But when you meet someone with that personality type for the first time, there's little chance of recognizing them for who they are – unless you're already familiar with someone similar.

The personality traits are difficult to diagnose due to their deceitful nature. Individuals with these traits are master manipulators and liars. They know how to tell you just what you want to hear.

On a personal level, constant lying and preoccupation with oneself are good indicators that someone has at least one of the dark triad traits. Still, it can be super hard to recognize a dark triad personality.

New research suggests that unstable parent-child relationships trigger attachment problems, significantly contributing to dark traits. A person with either of these traits may have been into physical, verbal, or sexual abuse or neglect in childhood. Additionally, genetic factors may make a person more predisposed to having the traits.

A few symptoms don't necessarily mean someone is expressing traits of the dark triad. As I said, they exist on a continuum; therefore, most people probably express the symptoms in varying degrees.

For example, you may have moments of entitlement, self-centeredness, or lack of empathy. If it is not an enduring or consistent experience, you most likely don't have any dark traits.

BEHAVIORS ASSOCIATED WITH DARK TRIAD

People with dark triad traits tend to behave aggressively out of self-promotion and a lack of empathy and remorse. Psychopathy and Machiavellianism have more similarities due to the predisposition for outrightly malicious behavior, whereas narcissism is more fragile and defensive.

But all three may exhibit the following symptoms:

- An unhealthy preoccupation with themselves.
- Lack of respect and empathy for others.
- A fascination with getting power by any means.
- Lying and manipulation.
- Violating social norms.
- Explosive anger.
- Potentially criminal behavior, such as stealing.
- Arrogance.
- A lack of remorse when they cause harm to others.
- An excessive need for praise and attention.

A 2017 research found that men generally have a score higher on the dark triad scale than women, particularly in psychopathy. This difference may be connected to antisocial behavior, one of the hallmark traits of psychopathy. It suggests that psychopathy is probably underlined by biological factors (testosterone) and social factors.

THE "D- FACTOR" SCALE

If you're eager to know how high you would score on the dark core scale, a nine-item test can give a reasonable estimate of where you'd fall on the scale. The stronger you agree with many items on this scale, the higher your likelihood of scoring high.

Strongly agreeing with just one item here doesn't mean you'd score high on the scale. But if you strongly agree with many things on the test, there's a high chance that you will have a high score.

1. One can't get ahead without cutting corners here and there.
2. I know I am special because people keep saying it.
3. Victims of mistreatment usually do something to deserve it.
4. I am more deserving than others.
5. I'll say or do anything to get what I want.
6. I make sure everyone knows about my successes.
7. I use clever manipulation to get what I want.
8. Hurting another person would be exciting and satisfying.
9. I don't mind experiencing pain or suffering to ensure others get the punishment they deserve.

Remember that this scale cannot be used to make an actual

diagnosis. It's to have a general idea of where you fall on the spectrum. You can take the authentic self-assessment created by the researchers who introduced the concept at http://qst.darkfactor.org.

THREE COMMONALITIES OF THE DARK TRIAD

There have been attempts to analyze the differences between narcissism, Machiavellianism, and psychopathy. To varying degrees, all three personalities act out of self-interest and a lack of empathy. They are skilled at deceiving and manipulating others, although with varying tactics and motivations. And they all operate in contrast to universal moral values and social norms.

As mentioned earlier, Machiavellianism and Psychopathy are more closely related in terms of malicious behavior. On the other hand, narcissists are fragile and defensive due to masked feelings of inadequacy.

All three personalities have low degrees of agreeableness (one of the Big Five personalities). Agreeableness is different from charisma or charms – which these types usually have in abundance. It involves straightforwardness, trustworthiness, compliance, modesty, kindness, and unselfishness, all essential for healthy and meaningful relationships.

Psychopaths and Machiavellians have lower conscientiousness than narcissists. Psychopaths have the lowest degree of negative emotions (neuroticism). Therefore, they are the most dangerous of all three personalities. Almost predictably, narcissists tend to be more extroverted and open. This matches evidence that they are usually creative.

Despite the common grounds, the dark triad personalities have significant differences, especially in why and how they do what they do. We will discuss this more when we get to the separate section on each personality type.

So, let's look at the three common traits in all the dark triad traits.

1. Deception

All three lack honesty, sincerity, humility, faithfulness, fairness, and lack of greed. Research on cheating found that the dark triad personalities cheat when there are low risks of getting caught. Even in high-risk circumstances, Machiavellians and psychopaths still cheat and deliberately lie. Meanwhile, narcissists tend to engage in self-deception rather than deliberate deception.

2. Callousness

For a deeper understanding of the lack of empathy among these personalities, researchers examined affective empathy – the ability to experience an appropriate emotional response to people's emotions – and cognitive empathy, the ability to determine others' emotional states.

The results showed that all three lacked affective empathy but possessed unimpaired cognitive empathy. Interestingly, they all feel positive emotions when others are in distress. Overall though, psychopaths and Machiavellians have the lowest empathy level. Narcissists typically have higher cognitive empathy than the other two personalities.

These personalities are insensitive to others' needs and feelings but retain the ability to evaluate others' emotions. This is how they can strategically exploit and manipulate people while unaffected by any harm they may cause.

3. Psychosocial consequences

All three dark personalities tend to engage in psychosocial behaviors such as bullying, lying, substance use, sexual harassment, infidelity, risk-taking, etc. But psychopaths are more predisposed to these behaviors than narcissists and Machiavellians.

The bottom line is those dark triad personalities are highly vicious, and people with these traits are likelier to use dark psychology tactics. They are expert manipulators and exceptional liars. So, you must learn how to spot them in any aspect of your life and avoid them. And if you already have someone like this, we will talk about the best approach to take in a subsequent chapter.

This chapter was meant as a brief introduction to the dark triad traits. In the following three chapters, we will explore the Dark Triad traits in-depth, identify their associated behaviors, and discuss how you can watch out for anyone with these traits.

Let's begin with narcissism.

CHAPTER 3:
Narcissism

The word "Narcissist" is prominent in popular culture. It gets tossed around in the celebrity-driven, social-media-obsessed culture as a description for anyone who seems arrogant and full of themselves. You might have used or heard "narcissist" or "narcissism" used to describe someone who:

- Appears vain and self-centered.
- Appears to only care about themselves.
- Exaggerate their accomplishments.
- Demand respect and attention from others
- Manipulate people for selfish ends.

But narcissism is widely misunderstood, leading to controversy about the condition. Some believe it is a choice of behavior, which it isn't. Others argue that narcissism is simply a personality type. I'm afraid none of these assumptions are correct.

Despite its origin in ancient Greek mythology, the term "narcissist" refers to people who exhibit traits of Narcissistic Personality Disorder (NPD), a personality disorder and life-limiting condition.

It's important to note this distinction because a personality disorder, like any mental health condition, shapes how a person thinks, feels, and behaves. In turn, this profoundly affects their everyday living and how they function at work, in relationships, and in general.

Most people exhibit at least one narcissistic behavior at some point. These narcissistic behaviors or attitudes are normal to an extent, but a personality disorder is more severe, lasts longer, and is frequent.

For example, good traits like generosity show in everyone to a greater or lesser degree. The same applies to narcissistic behavior.

Some aspects of narcissism could be a personality trait for some people. In others, these traits are so severe and intense that they permanently affect how these people interact with others and themselves.

Narcissism as a trait may sometimes appear in your behavior or thoughts. For example, suppose you have an ongoing row with a coworker. In that case, that might lead you to boast about your accomplishments or exaggerate the praise you get from your boss in front of this person. If this person is below you at work, you might even give them a poor review just to hurt them.

The behavior in the above example is an occasional reaction to that coworker rather than your general attitude toward everyone else. Therefore, that isn't a narcissistic disorder.

Narcissism in someone with a narcissistic personality disorder is persistent and characteristic. For example, your row might be with everyone at your workplace. It could be because you believe yourself more capable and intelligent than them.

This may have happened in your last job as well. Generally, you feel superior to most people you meet at work, school, and other places. Contrary to popular belief, a narcissist isn't someone who:

- Has high self-esteem
- Exhibits social confidence
- Is assertive
- Takes care of their physical appearance
- Is well-groomed
- Is competitive
- Proudly talks about their actual accomplishments or successes
- Dislikes you

Narcissism, like other dark traits, exists on a spectrum. It is distributed in the world population, with most people falling somewhere in the middle on the spectrum and a few at both extremes.

Some individuals may score somewhat high on the Narcissistic Personality Inventory (NPI), which may cause them to have an exceedingly charming disposition, especially when you first meet them, but come across as vain and shallow.

You may have awkward or stressful interactions with such individuals, but they still have fundamentally healthy personalities. So, they may have some degrees of narcissism without having a narcissistic personality disorder.

In a psychological context, true narcissists are preoccupied with an idealized, self-inflated version of themselves to avoid deep feelings of inadequacy and insecurity. Unfortunately, propping up their idealized self requires a lot of work, so they engage in dysfunctional behaviors and attitudes.

Narcissistic personality disorder (NPD) is marked by a pattern of self-centered thinking and behavior, an excessive need for external praise and admiration, and a lack of empathy for others. This pattern manifests in every aspect of a narcissist's life, including friendships, family, work, and intimate relationships.

Narcissists resist changing their behavioral patterns, even when it's detrimental to them. They tend to put the weight of their actions on other people. Moreover, they are extremely sensitive to criticism, disagreements, or perceived slights. They think of those as personal attacks.

Narcissists and Insecurity

The Diagnostic and Statistical Manual of Mental Disorders (DSM-5) reports that individuals with NPD typically have fragile self-esteem. Consequently, they spend a lot of time fixating on how others perceive them and whether they're doing well in life compared to others. This is insecurity, and it contributes to a narcissist's excessive need for admiration and praise.

Many narcissists struggle with insecurity and low self-esteem behind the facade of superiority they present to everyone else. But this is most common with covert or vulnerable narcissists.

People with the covert subtype of narcissism may display signs of insecurity and sensitivity to criticism or judgment. These are tied to the self-concept of being less than perfect and fuel stress, anxiety, depression, and other mental health concerns.

Such insecurity results in narcissists finding it hard to accept anything perceived as criticism in good faith. Critiques trigger feelings of vulnerability. For example, a narcissist may regard their supervisor's constructive feedback as a personal attack and react aggressively.

They might reply with contempt or drop a passive-aggressive remark about the supervisor. The purpose is to humiliate or reject the person who criticized them. Narcissists do it to prevent a potential threat to their outward mask of superiority.

Insecurity is a typical human trait. Everyone occasionally feels insecure or struggles with self-esteem issues, even without a mental health disorder. The key to discerning normal from narcissistic insecurity is the person's response to perceived threats. Responding with anger, rage, passive-aggression, or aggression strongly indicates narcissistic traits.

NARCISSISTIC TRAITS – HOW TO SPOT A NARCISSIST

It's pretty easy to label anyone who seems proud and vain, never doubts themselves, or spends much time talking about their accomplishments as a narcissist. However, spotting narcissism is a little more complex than that.

Narcissism isn't necessarily an overabundance of self-esteem. More accurately, the associated traits are:

- An unquenchable thirst for attention or admiration.
- A sense of entitlement to special treatment reflects the narcissist's perceived higher status.
- A constant desire for the spotlight.

Interestingly, research finds that many highly narcissistic individuals readily admit to being self-centered and attention-seeking.

If you're wondering whether someone in your life is a narcissist, you may be surprised to learn that the easiest way to figure it out is to ask them. We collectively assume that people don't realize they are narcissistic or will consider asking a challenge to their identity and, therefore, deny it.

However, in studies using the "Single-Item Narcissism Scale," individuals who answered yes to the singular question, "Are you a narcissist?" were more likely to score higher on the NPI.

Apart from this, there are other ways of spotting a narcissist or identifying narcissistic behavior. But before I get to that, let's briefly differentiate between the two subtypes of narcissism. These two share common traits but are underlined by different childhood experiences. This distinction dictates how the two types of narcissists behave in interpersonal interactions differently.

- **Grandiose Narcissism**

People with grandiose narcissism most likely had parents who treated them like they were superior to or above others in childhood. These expectations follow them into adulthood, molding them into arrogant elitists. They exhibit aggressiveness, dominance, and a tendency to exaggerate their importance. They aren't sensitive to criticism and are self-confident.

- **Vulnerable Narcissism**

This is often caused by neglect or abuse in childhood. Unlike grandiose narcissists, vulnerable narcissists are sensitive to criticism. They exhibit narcissistic behavior to shield themselves from deep-seated feelings of inadequacy. They may alternate between feeling superior and inferior to others but are deeply offended or anxious when they don't receive special treatment matching their perceived higher status.

Researchers are still studying and exploring narcissism, as most people with NPD rarely seek treatment independently. But there are common traits you may be able to spot in anyone with extremely high levels of narcissism, whether grandiose or covert.

Entitled behavior

Narcissists believe they are superior to others and, as such, deserve special treatment. They expect, and in many cases, demand that you should be obedient to their wishes. They also behave like rules and consequences don't apply to them.

Tendency to manipulate

A common trait of narcissism is controlling or manipulative behavior. At first, a narcissist will try to impress and please you to gain your confidence. But eventually, they start to put their needs first, even if it's at your expense. Narcissists try to maintain a distance to assert control when relating to others. They don't mind exploiting you for selfish purposes.

Need for praise and admiration.

One of the prevalent traits in narcissists is the constant expectation of praise and admiration. They have an insatiable need for validation from others. This pushes them to exaggerate or brag about their accomplishments for external validation and praise. Appreciation boosts their ego and allows them to keep up their facade.

A lack of empathy

Narcissists lack empathy, i.e., the ability to put themselves in others' shoes. If there's a narcissist in your life, they cannot bring themselves to empathize with your feelings, needs, or wants. This also makes it impossible to take personal responsibility for their actions. Instead, they deflect and blame other people for their behavior. *"You made me do it. I wouldn't have called you stupid otherwise."*

An exaggerated sense of self-importance

Narcissists believe they are superior to others. When they don't receive special treatment, they become rude or verbally abusive – usually toward those they consider inferior. Narcissists always tend to exaggerate their talents and achievements to put up the front of superiority. They are also preoccupied with fantasies of power, success, beauty, and brilliance.

Due to the exaggerated sense of self-importance, a narcissist typically believes they should only associate with perceived high-status of people.

Examples of Narcissistic Behavior

While there are many signs to help spot a narcissist, the ones we just discussed are usually enough for identifying narcissism in people. Still, it can be tricky. So, I have made a list of 5 behaviors that make it significantly easier to identify a narcissist when you meet.

The following are the most common examples of narcissistic behavior in people.

1. Monopolizing a conversation.

This is one of the most obvious examples of narcissistic behavior. Narcissists enjoy talking over or interrupting others to make their views known. They like nothing more than conversing about themselves, their experiences, or their supposed accomplishments.

A narcissist's tendency to monopolize conversations with others borders on compulsion. They will ignore whatever you say or respond superficially before redirecting the topic back to themselves.

This narcissistic behavior stems from the narcissist's need for praise, lack of empathy and respect, and exaggerated self-importance. These traits enable them to disregard your need to feel seen and heard. They would rather make themselves the center of attention.

2. Fixating on looks and appearance.

Narcissists are obsessed with their appearance, usually to an unhealthy degree. If you know anyone who spends hours in front of a mirror daily or constantly fixes their appearance in your presence, they're probably a narcissist.

Focusing on looks and appearance makes a narcissist more likely to discuss others' appearance. They may belittle you by criticizing your physical features, body type, or clothes.

Narcissists aren't just obsessed with physical appearance. They also have a preoccupation with how others perceive them. Consequently, they are particular about making grand impressions. They will even inflate or outrightly fabricate stories that make them seem more important than they are.

For narcissists, it's equally important for their lives to appear perfect and court admiration. Keeping up with the Joneses is one of the goals of a narcissistic parent. It's even better if they can surpass the Joneses.

3. Disregarding others' needs and feelings.

A narcissist may manipulate their interactions with others to further self-goals. They can cultivate intimate emotional relationships with someone to use that person's connection to boost their self-importance and benefit themselves.

Emotional manipulation by a narcissist often includes fierce arguments, intense mood swings, and a need to blame the other person for conflict. If a narcissist's family or partner becomes sick, they may neglect them at best or act mean at worst.

The lack of empathy makes it difficult for them to acknowledge others' pain or suffering.

4. "It's your fault."

It's always everyone else's fault when a narcissist makes a mistake or is caught doing something wrong. "Shame" and "blame" are critical tools in their arsenal – they use them to exert control. No matter what, a narcissist will find a way to one-up you. If you try to shake this power balance, the narcissist will do whatever is necessary to establish control.

Their favorite tactics to maintain or regain control include being rude, putting you down, making cruel jokes, criticizing, and sabotaging. For example, if you're insecure about a specific physical feature, you automatically become the butt of the narcissist's body-shaming jokes.

Sometimes, the narcissist lets go of the joke and comments rather bluntly. Since they cannot empathize, they may frame their comments as well-intended. If you protest, they will tell you it's for your good.

The narcissist uses the shaming tactic so that others can jump on the bandwagon. If that happens, you don't just face body-shaming from them, but the whole group.

5. There are always strings attached.

Any gift or help from a narcissist inevitably comes with strings attached. They use unsolicited gifts to manipulate you for their ends. Narcissists will never gift just for the sake of gifting – be it tangible or intangible, there are always strings attached to a narcissist's gift. When the time comes, they will come for their collateral.

Unfortunately, people with NPD act defensively about their character. They typically resist all attempts at an intervention. They are unwilling to seek treatment for their disorder. So, if you suspect there's a narcissist in your life or want to protect yourself from getting into a relationship with one, the best first step you can take is to know how to identify them.

"But what if I'm already in a narcissistic relationship based on suspicions?"

If you suspect anything like this, you're most likely a victim of narcissistic abuse. Find out what that means next.

ARE YOU A VICTIM OF NARCISSISTIC ABUSE?

A narcissistic relationship typically forms when one partner is highly narcissistic or struggles with Narcissistic Personality Disorder. Put, narcissists are terrible partners. They are more likely to engage in manipulative or exploitative behaviors and game-playing, inflicting narcissistic abuse on their partners.

If you're a fan of the sitcom Friends, you might be familiar with that episode where Chandler, one of the main characters, went on a date with a beautiful woman he met at Joey's stage play.

On the date, the woman went on and on about her experiences and adventures while Chandler listened. The poor guy could barely get a word in about himself. And then, just in time, she cut her ramblings short with the classic "But enough about me...."

When I think about narcissism, I often remember that particular scene. The woman may not have been a narcissist, but she exhibited narcissistic traits on the date.

If you have a partner who likes nothing more than to make everything about themselves, constantly needs attention, or seeks affirmation, you may be a victim of narcissistic abuse. They may be a narcissist if they believe they are always right or know more than you.

Narcissistic relationships can be significantly more challenging than other relationships. Narcissists don't truly love themselves. Therefore, it's difficult or even impossible for them to love another person. They are usually so preoccupied with themselves that they cannot truly "see" their partner as a separate individual with a distinct identity.

A narcissistic person only sees their lovers or friends in measure of how they fulfill their needs. You're only valued for your ability to meet their many demands and needs. Yet, many continue to be drawn to narcissistic relationships.

The thing about narcissists is they can be captivating, especially in

the early stages of a relationship. Most narcissists, if not all, have a "big" personality. They can make you feel like the luckiest person in the world for getting chosen by them. However, with time, their controlling nature comes to light. They get easily hurt. And when this happens, they lash out aggressively, cutting the other person deep.

Narcissists are driven by shame. They convince themselves of an idealized image and embody it so much that when the gap between their facade and their true selves shows, they feel a deep sense of shame. But they don't like that feeling, so they work extra hard to avoid it.

This also applies to codependent people, but narcissists employ destructive coping mechanisms that damage their loved one's self-esteem and relationships.

A narcissistic relationship can have you feeling very lonely. Your partner might treat you as an accessory, neglecting your needs and wants. They may constantly remind you that they're always right while you're wrong and incompetent.

You're left feeling angry and resentful and trying to defend yourself or internalizing the negative self-image and feeling bad about yourself. Naturally, this can decrease your self-esteem, leaving you even more vulnerable to narcissistic abuse.

Many of the narcissist's defense mechanisms are more on the abusive side, which is where the term "narcissistic abuse" comes from. Note that people can be abusive without being narcissistic.

Narcissistic abuse is a form of emotional, physical, or psychological abuse where the abuser uses their words and actions to manipulate their victim's emotional state and behavior. It occurs when a narcissist consistently manipulates and mistreats their partner to gain control and assert dominance over them. It involves vicious dark psychology techniques, such as love bombing, gaslighting, sabotaging, etc.

Abuse by a narcissist often comes in the form of criticism, accusations, threats, or put-downs. An abusive partner may withhold money, lie about you to others, or give you silent treatment. These are a few examples of manipulative techniques that make up their toolbox. Know that the end goal is to control your behavior so they can keep getting their narcissistic supply – an endless stream of attention and admiration needed to fuel their idealized self-image.

Signs of narcissistic abuse

Narcissistic abuse can be tough to detect, especially as narcissists approach potential victims with a charming, supportive, and kind exterior. However, there are signs one can watch for that can help identify narcissistic abuse. Here are six of those signs:

- **Feeling worthless or useless.**

Narcissistic abusers often work hard at damaging the self-esteem of their loved ones or romantic partners to create an environment where they are the person's only source of self-worth and validation.

Your partner might do this by constantly comparing you to others and telling you you don't measure up. This may lead to low self-esteem in your career, parenting, or friendships. Low self-esteem contributes to feelings of worthlessness and uselessness.

- **You no longer know who you are.**

After being subjected to the narcissist's manipulation and abuse, you may mold your identity to conform to your abuser's expectations. You do this because you are desperate for the relationship to continue.

Constantly accommodating yourself to another person's wants makes it harder to recognize yourself. You may no longer feel like yourself.

Some ways this manifest is changing your appearance to fit what your abuser wants, no longer doing things you enjoy because you want to make them happy, and finding it hard to identify your values, needs, and wants to separate from the narcissist.

- **Isolation from friends and family.**

An abusive partner will always try to isolate you from your support groups, including friends and family. It is a tactic to make you reliant on them and them alone. Eventually, you may stop contacting friends and family out of fear of angering the narcissist.

- **Physical changes.**

Narcissistic abuse can trigger stress and anxiety, which, in turn, trigger physical and physiological changes such as fatigue, muscle aches, pains, nausea, loss of appetite, migraine, etc.

As I said, narcissists can inflict abuse and suffering on their victims using specific manipulation tactics.

A NARCISSIST'S FAVORITE MANIPULATION TACTICS

Narcissists use manipulation tactics to subdue their victims and keep them in abusive relationships.

Love bombing

Love bombing is a narcissist's favorite tool. It involves overwhelming you with affection and adoration in the early phase of your relationship. A narcissist uses flattery and attention to gain your trust and convince you they are the perfect partner. They are skilled at donning the mask that will attract you to them the most.

Gaslighting

A narcissistic partner deliberately makes you distrust your view of reality, even convincing you that you're mentally incompetent. They do this by denying when something happens, questioning the validity of your memory, or trivializing how you feel. For example, suppose you catch them looking into your phone without permission. The narcissist might insist that's not what happened even though you caught them in the act. They will keep up the denial so much that

you might start to doubt if you hallucinated the event.

Devaluing

Your abusive partner might dismiss your accomplishments or worth and belittle, insult, degrade, or humiliate you. They do this to tear at your self-esteem – that way, they become the only ones who can make you feel good about yourself and weaponize that.

Intimidation

A narcissist may use aggression, bullying, and other intimidating behaviors to maintain control in the relationship.

Narcissistic Rage

Sometimes, the narcissist uses sudden attacks of unbridled rage that can cause the victim physical harm or mental distress.

Emotional Blackmail

They may threaten to leave you, harm themselves, or take other drastic actions if you don't behave the way they want or try to leave the relationship. Emotional blackmail gets you to conform to their demands to your detriment.

Negative Contrasting

Your narcissistic partner may unnecessarily compare you to themselves or others in unflattering ways. Again, they do this to eat at your self-esteem and leave you feeling worthless.

Withholding

They might withhold sex, money, affection, or communication from you.

Lying and Denial

Your partner may bombard you with lies regularly. When you catch them in a lie, they either deny or tell another lie to cover it up.

Privacy Invasion

They may ignore or violate your boundaries by going through your phone, mail, and other things; stalking or following you everywhere; ignoring your requests for privacy no matter how many times you ask.

Slander

If things somehow come to an end or you start to show signs of leaving the relationship, your abuser might spread malicious gossip and lies about you to friends, family, and anyone who cares to hear.

Financial Abuse

Narcissists often try to control their partner or victim through financial domination. They might extort you for money or, in some cases, commit outright theft. Narcissists often accrue debt in their partner's money and sell the partner's property or possessions.

Isolation

They isolate you from friends, family, and other sources of support through slander, verbal abuse, control, and other means of abuse.

Violence

In some cases, the narcissist resorts to physical violence by throwing things, pulling hair, blocking movement, or destroying property.

The severity of abuse in a narcissistic relationship can range from ignoring your needs to physically harming you. Don't expect a narcissist to take the blame for their actions – they have mastered the art of shifting blame from themselves to other people.

DEALING WITH NARCISSISTS

Navigating any relationship with a narcissist can be extremely distressing and frustrating. A narcissistic relationship will leave your self-esteem damaged and your perception of reality impaired.

Communicating or arguing with a narcissist about their actions will likely prove fruitless. The best way to handle narcissists is to establish personal boundaries and set consequences for when they violate them.

When boundaries aren't enough, your next best strategy is emotionally distancing yourself from them. You may not be able to control how you feel about a narcissistic partner or friend, but you can dictate how you act on those feelings.

Cutting ties with a narcissistic partner, friend, boss, or family member is usually the best way to deal with them. It may be the only solution sometimes. In the process, it would be best to reflect on the narcissist's characteristics to avoid finding yourself in a similar relationship.

The most important thing is to know as much as possible about all the tactics narcissists use to manipulate and control others. So, we will look more closely at those techniques discussed in a subsequent chapter about manipulation tactics.

Let's talk about Machiavellianism, another dark triad personality that utilizes malevolent dark psychology tactics to manipulate and control unsuspecting people.

CHAPTER 4:
Machiavellianism

Ever met someone who is always scheming and plotting? Maybe someone who believes every situation is an opportunity to exploit for self-advancement? Perhaps a person who is so manipulative that you wonder how they got so good at it?

Whether you've met someone like that or only seen it in movies, chances are you are familiar with these traits.

In the 16th century, Niccolo Machiavelli, a political adviser, and philosopher, published "The Prince," a document in which he asserted that deception, cunning, and wickedness are more important traits for political leaders than virtue and morality. He said, "It is more important to be feared than loved."

This is the origin of the word "Machiavellian," which describes anyone with the traits Machiavelli glorified in his manifesto. Then, in the 1970s, Richard Christie and Florence Geiss formally introduced Machiavellianism as a personality trait characterized by manipulativeness, deceit, and cynicism.

A Machiavellian is manipulative, cunning, and driven to gain power by any means possible. They are calculating and strategic. When a Mach has a goal, they devise a thorough plan to achieve it without considering how it might affect others involved.

They use manipulation, exploitation, and deception to get whatever they want, often coming off as cold and unemotional. This personality type is prevalent in men but can affect anyone at any age.

When interacting with a high Mach, as psychologists call them, you might find them charming and engaging. Still, it's difficult to feel "close" to them. This is probably due to their lack of empathy.

Unlike narcissists, Machiavellians seek to achieve their goals without making themselves the center of attention. They do not need your admiration or praise. They are OK with pulling the strings behind the curtain.

Their cynical view of others drives Machiavellians. They only care about using others to their advantage. As such, they are skilled at manipulating others for selfish reasons without caring about possible consequences. The result of this is that they are inclined to shallow emotional experiences.

You might meet a high Mach capable of forming some emotional attachment, but your relationship will likely be abusive and dysfunctional. No matter how long you've had a relationship, they are ready to walk away as soon as you no longer benefit them.

Most high Machs suffer from alexithymia, which is the inability to feel emotions. Consequently, they tend to be out of touch with their feelings. According to Psychologists Christie and Geis, Machs don't form real bonds with others; therefore, they cannot form genuine, meaningful relationships.

They are selfish and indifferent to conventional moral or ethical values. At their worst, high Machs only care about money, power, and control and are willing to do anything for all three. They care little for self-care, family community, or community building. Their foremost goal in life is to win at any cost consistently.

A person who scores high on the Machiavellian test may not necessarily be a political leader or hold a formal position of power but use strategic calculating to boost their self-worth. They are naturally skilled at influencing others with the primary goal of exploiting opportunities for personal power.

There may be some genetic predisposition toward Machiavellian traits. However, they are probably caused by early parental influences and upbringing. A bad childhood can shape a person's personality toward Machiavellianism.

For some, it could be a maladaptive coping strategy formed from

living in conditions where the Mach needed those traits to survive no matter what.

Not all Machs are equally good at plotting and scheming their way to power or success. Some are smart, and some aren't – the smart ones usually climb up the corporate or political ladder, whereas the not-so-smart ones end up in the prison system or, worse, in jail.

Often, the ones who make it in the corporate world use people so much that they end up with plenty of enemies. Being Machiavellian and not building true, collaborative relationship is a poor strategy. Some are skilled strategists that know how to use cooperation to their advantage.

There are many ways to recognize a Machiavellian. According to empirical research, these are some sure ways to spot a Mach, especially in your workplace.

1. They don't express a full range of emotions and often appear detached. Machs derive pleasure from watching distressing events unfold. They don't display negative affect, no matter the situation.
2. They perform well in competitive environments. In the workplace, Machs may appear friendly and charming at first. That is because they use a gentle approach to gain people's commitment. But, over time, you might notice how inauthentic and competitive they are. They don't mind costing a coworker their job to gain favor with the boss.
3. They thrive in ambiguity. Machiavellians rarely do well in rule-based environments because they thrive in places where

the rules are ambiguous, and they can bend them to fit their ambition. They tend to ignore the standards of rule-based institutions repeatedly.
4. They try to minimize others' influence by withholding knowledge from coworkers. They don't cooperate but compete even when they are in a team.
5. They might entice coworkers to behave in risky ways or try to seduce supervisors and coworkers into intimate relationships for their ends.

It's not helpful to label people but watching out for these signs can help you identify a Machiavellian personality.

HALLMARK TRAITS OF A MACHIAVELLIAN

Machiavellians generally have the following traits and behaviors among a myriad of individual traits.

Manipulativeness

Machiavellians will lie, cheat, flatter, and do whatever it takes to get their way. They have a talent for reading people and using their limitations against them. They bend the rules, use trickery, and fake sympathy to court favors. At first, they may be charming, but in time, they resort to aggressive tactics, such as intimidating and bullying. They are morally lacking and willing to cause others harm to meet their ends.

Lack of empathy

Because these predators are emotionally detached, they cannot empathize with people's feelings or needs. They have zero care for how their actions might impact you. This contributes to their willingness to do whatever is necessary to accomplish their goals. Despite their manipulative tendencies, Machs are usually less emotionally intelligent. They also lack compassion.

Self-interest

I mentioned that Machs have a cynical view of everyone. As a result, they believe everyone acts out of self-interest like them. This is one reason why they find it difficult to trust or form close relationships with other people. It also makes them incredibly disloyal, as their cynical approach leads them to dismiss social pacts or bonds of trust.

An obsession with personal power

Another hallmark trait of Machiavellianism is how easily they throw others under the bus for personal advancement. Personal fulfillment is the most important thing to a Mach, and it can come in the form of praise, power, or other forms of glory – as they call it.

Deceit

Machiavellians understand the importance of information. They often withhold information from others unless it would benefit them to do the opposite. They tend to manipulate otherwise harmless information and habitually take things out of context for personal gain.

Competitiveness

As I noted, Machs are incredibly competitive, so they consider everyone an adversary. They are only willing to be a team player or take a back seat if it is to their advantage. Their sensitivity to the power dynamics in social situations makes it easy for them to switch from cooperative to competitive and vice versa.

Ambition

Machs have high ambitions and are willing to manipulate and control their way to achieving them. Power and ambition amplify the Machiavellian's natural behavioral dispositions, beliefs, and emotions.

A MACHIAVELLIAN'S FAVORITE MANIPULATION TACTICS

A Machiavellian personality may employ various manipulation techniques to achieve their goals. Some of their favorites include:

Charm

Using compliments, flattery, and praise to make you feel important or unique. Machiavellians are often charismatic and persuasive. They use their charm to win you over, making you more susceptible to influence and control.

Deception

The machiavellian know how to deceive people to gain an

advantage. They may use lies, half-truths, and information withholding to manipulate your perception or understanding of a situation.

Strategic information control

As mentioned earlier, Machiavellians understand the value of information. Therefore, they may conceal or selectively disclose information to manipulate how others perceive a situation, control the narrative, or gain an advantage. They use information as leverage.

Creating division

They may deliberately create conflict or division among teams or individuals to weaken them and assert or maintain dominance. They are skilled at exploiting tension and fostering mistrust, allowing them to manipulate others to serve their interest.

Exploiting weaknesses

Unlike narcissists and psychopaths, Mach's plots and schemes. They don't mind taking as long as needed to observe other people's limitations or vulnerabilities keenly. Then, they use that knowledge to manipulate, exploit, or blackmail them.

Threats

When necessary, they may use fear, guilt, and intimidation tactics to influence other people's behaviors and decisions.

Overall, Machs keenly understand human nature and how to maneuver it to their advantage. The brilliant ones can accurately assess someone else's motives, desires, and vulnerabilities, enabling them to take a practical calculating approach to any situation.

COPING WITH MACHIAVELLIANS

The best option for coping with a Machiavellian does not have to cope with them at all. In other words, cut them off, and don't accept anyone with similar traits into your life. However, if you cannot cut off the Mach in your life, these tips can help you cope with them.

- **Don't take their behavior personally.** Whether the Mach is a friend, partner, or coworker, dealing with them can leave you insecure, angry, used, or disappointed. It would be best not to personalize their behavior, thinking something must be wrong with them. Accept that their actions reflect them, not you.
- **Limit your interactions.** If you know anyone with Machiavellian traits, limiting your interactions is best to protect your peace. Do not partake in any game with them or try to outsmart them. Don't try to get them back for something they did. You may end up with the shorter stick. The best thing you can do is to avoid them as much as possible.
- **Manage your vulnerabilities.** If a Mach has already taken advantage of you once or twice, do not self-blame or act vulnerable. That'll only open up another chance for them to manipulate your emotions and weaknesses. Instead, seek out your support system and express your feelings to them in a safer space.

- **Stick to a work-focused topic.** If you suspect your coworker is a Machiavellian personality, limit interactions with them as much as possible. But if you have to talk to them, do everything to keep the conversations on work-related topics. They will try to charmingly steer you to talk about your personal life or struggles – don't take the bait. Remind yourself that they only want to make you vulnerable to obtaining personal information that makes it easier to prey on you. For example, if they invite you to drink together after work, tell them you cannot make it. Don't give an explanation or excuse – you can't make it.
- **Establish a win-win outcome if you can.** If you ever get in a competition or tricky situation with a Machiavellian, it's best to give them a win-win outcome. Machs are focused on achieving positive outcomes for themselves and usually don't care if you win too. Give them a win if you can while keeping your focus on your goals.
- **Surround yourself with those you trust and count on for support.** If you haven't already, they can help you see the Mach for who they are. Furthermore, your support system can provide the resources and motivation you need to end your relationship with the Mach.
- **Practice self-care and self-compassion.** Machs have no consideration for others' feelings and needs. Prioritize your physical, emotional, and personal needs through a daily self-care routine. Even if they ignore your needs, try to meet them yourself.

Psychologists don't recommend having any form of relationship with Machiavellians. They are hardwired to manipulate and will take any opportunity to do that, no matter how close you think you are with them.

Despite your efforts to change them, their behaviors and manipulative tendencies are deeply ingrained. That makes them highly resistant to any form of personal adjustments or growth. And if you recommend seeking professional help, they will most likely turn down that offer.

Again, the best way to cope with a Machiavellian personality is not to get involved with them on any level.

We've discussed the first two Dark Triad personalities in-depth. Now, it's time to examine the third and final personality type, psychopathy. Here's one thing you should know before we proceed to the next chapter: Psychopaths are significantly worse than Narcissists and Machiavellians – whew, I know, right!

CHAPTER 5:
Psychopathy

"Some people try to be tall by cutting off the heads of others."

– Paramahansa Yogananda.

Psychopath. You hear this word, and your mind immediately conceives images of criminals, violent offenders, murderers, and serial killers. Nobody thinks of an ordinary person when they hear the word "psychopath." Yet, there are plenty of psychopaths in our lives, at work, in school, and in the community. Most people know the term, but few know what it truly means.

The word "psychopath" describes a callous, emotionally detached, and morally depraved individual. A lack of empathy and impairment of other affective states characterizes psychopathy.

Although psychopathy isn't an official mental health condition or diagnosis, it is recognized as a trait in individuals who are typically antisocial, egocentric, lacking empathy and remorse, and crime-leaning.

Psychopaths often have a typical, charming exterior. Beneath that, they have no conscience or moral scruples. Their antisocial nature usually predisposes them to criminal behavior, but not always.

Though confident and charismatic, the psychopath is narcissistic and immoral. As such, he operates with no restraint in getting what he wants. At first, he may don a charming facade, but he flips easily and without warning or provocation to cunning, dangerous, and cruel.

Unlike a typical narcissist, the psychopath doesn't just take a transactional approach to interpersonal relationships and uses people for what they can do. And yes, there are more male than female psychopaths.

In this age, the modern psychopath is rarely the mass murderer portrayed in the media. Instead, he is usually outwardly functional and successful. He manipulates and instigates harm toward his victims using indirect but insidious means.

The psychopath entices people with his superficial and calculated charm in the early phase of a personal relationship. Then, he unleashes his callous and uncaring nature after an agreement or commitment is established.

Psychopaths manipulate, deceive, and abuse people without remorse. Victims of psychopaths are often left injured and traumatized by the utter void of empathy and decency.

In professional relationships, high-functioning psychopaths are ambitious, intelligent, exploitative, ruthless, and aggressive. Like Machiavellians, they maneuver their way to powerful positions in finance, business, media, politics, and other fields of higher status.

Like other Dark Triad traits, psychopathy exists on a continuum; therefore, psychopathic behavior varies significantly from one person to another. Some psychopaths are violent offenders and murderers, whereas others are highly successful leaders. The difference lies in the traits.

A person can exhibit psychopathic traits in varying degrees without being a psychopath. Usually, individuals with psychopathic traits don't exhibit psychopathic behavior. Those with psychopathic traits and behavior are often diagnosed with Antisocial Personality Disorder (ASPD).

Early research suggests that psychopathy often stems from parent-child attachment issues. Parental rejection, emotional deprivation, and a lack of affection are all believed to increase the risk of a child becoming psychopathic in adulthood.

The early onset of behavioral problems is a predictive variable of psychopathy. Most psychopaths steal, cheat, and display similar behaviors at a young age and are likely to engage in them throughout their lives.

A psychopath's low capacity for empathy and remorse leads them to disregard the feelings and health of those they victimize, usually with a lack of guilt.

Connections are essential to the psychopath. Due to the insatiable need for power and control, every individual the psychopath connects to is seen as an end – someone who can serve his needs in various ways.

Some experts suggest that narcissism and psychopathy are on the same spectrum and have low degrees of agreeableness. Yet only psychopaths also have low degrees of conscientiousness.

So, how can you spot such a possibly dangerous individual from genuinely charming and charismatic people?

CORE TRAITS OF PSYCHOPATHY

In a nutshell, these core traits should let you know when a psychopath is in your environment or trying to wiggle into your life.

Pathological lying and manipulativeness.

Know the saying, "If you repeat a lie often enough, it becomes the truth?" That is what psychopaths embody. In pursuit of power and control, psychopaths will tell blatant lies, distort the truth, deceive, break promises, and blame others when caught in a lie. Pathological lying is a core trait of psychopathy.

Not only do they lie to get out of trouble, but they also do it to look good. They tell more lies to cover up previous lies. This makes it hard to keep their stories straight as they often forget what they've said.

If challenged, a psychopath will deny or dismiss your evidence with contempt. Or he will change the story and rework the facts.

Superficial charm

Psychopaths, especially the high-functioning ones, are usually likable. They are great conversationalists and typically have lots of stories to share with others, most of which are meant to make them look good. They may also be fun and charismatic.

The seeming charms make it relatively easy for unsuspecting people to fall prey to psychopathic individuals.

Need for the thrill (stimulation)

Psychopaths crave excitement. They want constant thrill in their lives, making them live in the "fast lane." Often, a psychopath will seek stimulation by breaking the rules or laws. They may seek the thrill of getting away with a crime or rule-breaking. They may even engage in criminal activities just for the thrill of "getting caught" at any moment. Consequently, they cannot tolerate routines or partake in dull, repetitive tasks.

Shallow affect

Psychopaths have a severe form of antisocial personality disorder. As such, they are emotionally detached. They cannot portray vulnerable emotions – if they do, it's sure to be fake. They may come off as cold, unemotional, and calculating much of the time. But if it serves a purpose to their ends, they can show a dramatic range of emotions. Unfortunately, a discerning mind can usually tell that these are shallow performances.

Lack of empathy and remorse

Psychopaths are incapable of putting themselves in others' shoes. They struggle to empathize with people who are afraid, anxious, or sad. As a result, they are numb to people's suffering – even when it's their loved ones.

At the same time, they don't care about the impact of their behavior on other people. They rarely remember how their actions might have hurt someone. If you express your hurt feelings, they will dismiss it as an overreaction.

Ultimately, psychopaths are unaffected by the pain and suffering they cause others. They justify their actions and blame others for being "stupid" or "weak." Remember that this is common with narcissists and Machiavellians too.

Impulsivity

A psychopath will rarely consider the potential benefits and risks of something before making a choice. They have little to no control over their impulses. Instead, they seek instant gratification. So, they may end a relationship, quit their job, buy a new home or car, or move to a new country on a whim – with zero consideration for the people in their lives.

False superiority complex

Most psychopaths have narcissistic traits, but not all narcissists are psychopathic. Fake charm, self-absorption, entitlement, manipulativeness, and a false sense of superiority are some narcissistic traits psychopaths also have.

In the mind of many psychopaths, they are "better" than others and therefore reserve the right to mistreat and take advantage of them at will. They treat those they deem inferior with contempt.

Other traits of a psychopath include:
- Poor behavioral controls
- Promiscuity
- Perversive sexual behavior
- Lack of realistic, long-term goals

- Irresponsibility
- Criminal versatility

Examples of well-known psychopaths in real life include Charles Manson, Ted Bundy, Jack the Ripper, etc. Meanwhile, examples of fictional psychopaths include Cersei Lannister, Hannibal Lecter, Joffrey Baratheon, Patrick Bateman, etc.

HOW PSYCHOPATHS MANIPULATE

One of the defining traits of psychopaths is the tendency to manipulate others through lying, deception, and superficial charm. If you've ever encountered a psychopathic individual in the short or long term, your experience probably left you feeling deceived, used, and hurt. You might also feel a bit foolish for falling prey to the psychopath.

It's possible that the psychopath manipulated and deceived you just for the fun of it or to get something from you. However, many also do it because they can't control the impulse to take advantage of others.

The core traits of a psychopath develop over a lifetime, usually through habit and reinforcement. As such, they are incapable of changing their ways.

Recognizing that you're being manipulated is always the first step to avoiding the emotional trap a psychopath may be set for you.

In your first meeting, a psychopath uses impression management techniques because they understand that humans are hardwired to size each other up.

Various factors, such as attractiveness, facial shape, emotional state, vocal inflection, etc., influence first impressions. We tend to get attached to our first impressions of others, making it hard to change our perspective even when evidence to the contrary arises.

Psychopaths are aware of this. Therefore, they deliberate how they come across to others on a first meeting. As a result, they use impression management techniques – modulating negative traits and accentuating their strengths – to ensure you form a favorable opinion of them.

They adjust everything from posture to clothing style and conversational style to make a great first impression.

Unfortunately, people use subtle facial and vocal clues to judge a person's physical strength, trustworthiness, and intentions to harm. It would be best if you learned to see through these techniques to keep a psychopath away from you.

In short, knowing the ways psychopaths manipulate can help you learn to resist better or avoid them. Here are some of their favorite tactics:

- **The facade:** Psychopaths put on a mask of deception to make themselves more likable, charming, and agreeable. Consequently, there's always a smile on their face and witty remarks so close to their lips.
- **Persuasion:** Psychopaths are skilled at talking people out of their values and moral standards with "logic." They know how to convince others to partake in immoral activities for their ends by making it seem like no big deal.
- **Deception:** A psychopath might make up stories that never happened to make themselves appear more attractive, learned, valuable, or experienced. At the same time, they might downplay or dismiss things that make them look bad. Another thing they do is reveal made-up "secrets" about themselves to make themselves more likable or trustworthy.
- **Evading questions:** If the true answer to a question would put a psychopath further behind in achieving their desired goal, they might change the subject subtly or speak in

broader terms to tiptoe their way around it. This is a tactic they commonly use to distort the truth.

Under the right circumstances, a psychopath may perceive themselves as honest or sincere, but this won't stop them from trying to manipulate or deceive you.

COPING WITH A PSYCHOPATH

Most psychopaths are aversive to treatment because they don't see anything wrong. They convince themselves that others are wrong. As a result, the people in their lives have to find effective strategies for coping with a psychopath. After all, having such a callous, emotionally detached person in your life can be difficult.

Whether the psychopath in your life is a friend, family member, boss, or lover, their behavior can severely impair your psychological well-being if you aren't careful. The best way to cope with a psychopath is to limit or cut off contact with them. If you can't do that, you need to establish healthy boundaries and enforce them.

Now that we've discussed all three dark triad traits, their different characteristics, and manipulative tendencies, it's time to talk about manipulation and its many forms.

CHAPTER 6:
Manipulation

Manipulation involves using covert tactics to control emotions, behavior, and relationships. It happens in various relationship dynamics, from romantic partnerships to friends, family, and professional relationships. Everyone has manipulative tendencies, yet they can be incredibly hard to recognize.

Imagine a beautiful garden, wherein lies a spider, carefully weaving an intricate web. The spider spins its web to entrap unsuspecting prey. This is how manipulation works – an intricate web of dark psychology tactics.

A manipulator delicately constructs their words and actions to create an illusion of influence. The thoughts, feelings, and behaviors of anyone ensnared in the manipulator's web of lies and manipulative techniques become twisted and distorted from reality.

Similarly, to how the spider preys on unsuspecting victims, manipulators prey on the vulnerable, leaving them a tangled mess of shattered trust and broken self-esteem.

Manipulation is often so subtle and effective that the victim questions their perception of the situation rather than the manipulator's actions and motives. Most people manipulate others from time to time. For example, if you tell a friend you're "not that fine" to make them come to your apartment after they said they couldn't, that's technically manipulation.

Manipulative behavior influences or controls other people's perceptions of you and their reactions toward you. It can happen consciously or subconsciously, often without ill intentions.

Though typically viewed negatively, manipulation isn't always a bad skill. Sometimes, manipulation is used to influence others to work toward a goal. However, when a person uses manipulation tactics to coerce rather than persuade, it becomes toxic and even dangerous in some situations.

We see manipulation everywhere in society. It's in every advertisement, prevalent on social media, and a regular part of our everyday interactions. Social manipulation produces positive interpersonal interactions, such as using common interests to get a person to open up.

There are many benefits of utilizing manipulation as a form of persuasion. It can help people open up or influence them to compromise in specific situations. Parents are encouraged to use positive manipulation tactics to influence their kids' behavioral outcomes. All of these are examples of beneficial social influence.

In any relationship with healthy social influence, there is always a give and take, which is constructive and contributes to the relationship's health.

But there is a more insidious side to manipulation. As a fully functional human being, you have unique thought processes that aren't easy to control. Your wants, needs, interests, and preferences guide you through life.

When someone else tries to dictate or control your choices without your explicit permission, they might turn to emotional and psychological manipulation.

The critical difference between manipulation as a form of healthy social influence and psychological manipulation is that there is a power imbalance, and one person is exploited and used to serve the other person's agenda.

Emotional manipulation is "a form of psychological manipulation in which an individual seeks to control someone else's emotions." It is often achieved through persuasion, coercion, and emotional blackmail in some cases.

This side of manipulation creates power struggles in relationships and cultivates a toxic, abusive environment. When manipulation becomes coercive, it subtly forces people into thoughts, actions, and choices against their will.

Understanding why people manipulate is crucial in protecting yourself from manipulators.

WHY PEOPLE MANIPULATE

On the surface, manipulation is an apparent attempt at getting what one wants. But from a psychological perspective, behaviors are a wide range of factors. The overarching theme of psychological manipulation is always about power and control.

Manipulators need power and control over any situation or relationship which drives them. For some, emotional manipulation becomes habitual and ingrained due to past trauma. Some individuals who experience abuse in childhood turn into manipulators because they can't express their feelings and needs directly in healthy ways without being punished.

Others are manipulative because they were raised in an environment where it was normal behavior and didn't learn healthier ways of communicating their needs and wants.

Then, you have those such as the dark triad personalities who manipulate because of a mental health condition impairing their behavior. These people use manipulation to control others for personal leverage, a need to have an advantage, or a desire to feel better than the people in their lives.

Manipulators who crave power and control resort to scheming to achieve their objectives. They exploit others' emotions to domineer them and exhibit dramatic emotions for attention-seeking ends, mainly when a situation is out of their control.

Consequently, devious manipulators avoid situations they can't control since it's harder to create predictable outcomes that align with their wants and goals.

They may have started using manipulation tactics for survival, self-preservation, or in response to deep-seated feelings of inadequacy. Still, their behaviors can spiral to the point where they disrupt a healthy, functional relationship. That is how they create toxic and unhealthy interpersonal relationships, and their behaviors become pathological over time.

Understanding what drives manipulation is vital to identifying manipulative behavior and taking the proper steps to protect yourself or stop a manipulator. Only when you understand manipulators can you truly intervene to meet their needs in healthier ways or end your relationship with them, if necessary.

SIGNS AND EXAMPLES OF PSYCHOLOGICAL MANIPULATION

Many don't even recognize when someone is trying to confuse or control them. You may get that feeling of unease in your gut. The manipulator says one thing, but you're feeling something entirely different. Or you feel like you've been trapped into agreeing with the manipulator's request or demand. Yet, you dismiss it and ignore it.

Consequently, you may react in a way that escalates abuse or play into the abuser's hand. If you grew up with manipulative parents, it could be harder to recognize manipulation in others – especially a romantic partner – since the behavior feels familiar.

"Know thy enemy." This ancient wisdom should be everyone's number one tool when dealing with a manipulator. Recognizing signs of being manipulated enables you to respond strategically to overt or covert manipulation. It empowers you.

Here, we will look at a list of "tricks" manipulators often use to put others at a disadvantage. This isn't an exhaustive list, but it can give you insight into manipulators' behavior.

It would be best if you were familiar with these signs and examples of psychological manipulation to recognize them whenever your

rights or safety is at stake.

- **You experience distressing emotions.**

Every interaction with a manipulator trigger overriding negative emotions. Anxiety, fear, and guilt are some of the emotions you feel when interacting with that person. A fear of what to expect torments you. How will they act? What will they do to get what they want?

Guilt becomes a familiar feeling, and you feel it arise anytime you do something contrary to the manipulator's desires or express your opinion. Psychological manipulation is meant to coerce you into doing things against your will. Therefore, you may also have a sense of obligation to the manipulator.

This includes a sense that you're accountable to this person and should act or think according to their preferences and inclinations.

- **You question your reality.**

This happens as a result of the manipulation tactic known as gaslighting. Constantly questioning your memory or perception of interaction with the person is a sign that you're being gaslighted.

Gaslighting also involves being told that what you see right before your eyes isn't true. Or being made to feel that a situation was your fault.

Psychological manipulators also double as master gaslighters. They are skilled at lying, denying, making excuses, and distorting facts to misrepresent the reality of a situation. All of these can make you start questioning your reality.

- **You get blamed for everything.**

Manipulators do not take responsibility for their actions unless it gives them an advantage. Neither do they take the blame for adverse outcomes in their relationships. Therefore, the manipulative individual in your life will blame you for everything wrong. Sometimes, they may blame other people for their feelings and actions instead of owning them.

If you find yourself in a dynamic where you're constantly forced to be the bigger person or apologize to "keep the peace," that's a strong indicator that there is a pattern of psychological manipulation.

- **Your feelings are minimized.**

The manipulator degrades you at every turn. You can get nothing right and exist under a microscopic lens. This individual verbally devalues you at every opportunity, highlighting your perceived flaws, not just to you but others. They ensure you hear their opinions loudly and clearly over the opinions of others.

- **Every disagreement is a generalization or an ultimatum.**

"You never listen," "You always act like this," and "If you can't give me what I want, I will leave" – these are some of a manipulator's favorite sentences. They generalize and give ultimatums to induce feelings of fear and guilt that can produce their desired outcome.

Rather than address each situation on its own merits, manipulators generalize to keep the situation ambiguous and confuse you, making it harder to pinpoint their behaviors occurring beneath the surface.

Examples of manipulative behavior:
- "If you truly loved me, you wouldn't accuse me of that."
- "You never treat me right."

- "You'd rather choose your friends over me?"
- "If you ever do that again, you will regret the day we met."
- "You made me hit you!"
- "We can go on a date when you burn some calories."
- "I know you're cheating on me."

Psychological manipulation is a pattern of abuse, especially if consistent and paired with different forms of emotional manipulation.

COVERT MANIPULATION TACTICS TO KNOW

Manipulation often includes overt aggression in the form of

criticism, subtle emotional abuse, and narcissistic abuse. It also includes covert tactics such as lying, denial, mind games, emotional blackmail, flattery, etc. Common tactics are described below:

Lying & Denial

Compulsive and pathological liars tend to lie even when it's unnecessary. They don't lie out of fear or guilt but to create confusion. Some combine lying with accusations to put you on the defensive.

Lying sometimes happens indirectly – for example, they may omit a vital piece of information or give you vague details, though everything else is true. For example, a cheating partner might lie that they were working late without admitting to something else they did.

Denial occurs together with lying. This isn't the kind of denial used to avoid facing difficult situations. Instead, it's deliberate denial to discredit knowledge of agreements, promises, or behavior. It also included minimizing or rationalizing their behavior with excuses and justifications.

They may act like you're blowing the situation out of proportion, excuse their actions to gain your sympathy, or make you doubt yourself.

Avoidance

Manipulators avoid confrontations that can lead to them taking responsibility for their choices or actions at all costs. They may refuse to have discussions about their behavior. This is usually paired with an attack to put you on the defensive with guilt, blame, or shame. *"You're always breathing down my neck."*

It's hard to notice this tactic due to the subtlety of a manipulator changing the subject. It may be hidden behind a compliment, boasting, or something they know you want to hear. For example, *"You know I love you so much, right?"* makes you forget the reason for the conversation in the first place.

Intimidation

The manipulator may not threaten you directly. Sometimes, they do it with their tone of voice, a menacing look, and statements like: *"You are replaceable,"* *"Have you considered the possible consequences of that choice,"* *"I know powerful people,"* or *"I always get my way."*

Another strategy is telling you a fear-provoking story, such as *"I know a woman who once left her husband. She lost the house, their kids, and everything. She's homeless now."*

Guilt-Tripping

Ever had someone try to make you feel guilty for your decision or choice? That is guilt-tripping. It often involves the manipulator using something they did for you or something you did against them as leverage to get what they want. Example: *"If you can't come over, I might as well spend the weekend alone. No point inviting anyone else then."*

Projection

Projection happens when a manipulator attributes an emotion they're feeling, such as jealousy, to someone else. It is used to dodge responsibility and avoid changing their behavior. The downside is it creates distrust in your reality.

Note: Be careful not to project your values onto the manipulator, as that will only set you up for disappointment and heartache.

Flattery

It can be hard to discern a compliment from flattery. A compliment is a sincere remark on something positive given with no expectation of personal gain. Flattery, on the other hand, is a tool for gaining emotional leverage – there's always an expectation of gain.

For instance, a coworker who likes to dump their work on you might regularly praise your skills, strengths, and accomplishments.

Playing the Victim

Instead of blaming you, the manipulator might use a "poor me" strategy to evoke feelings of guilt and sympathy to get their wanted outcome. *There's nothing I can do if you don't help me.* A manipulator with a mental disorder might threaten suicide to get you to stay.

Isolation

Your manipulator knows there's safety in numbers, so they work hard to isolate you from your loved ones and everyone you feel comfortable around. Once they achieve this, it's easier to control and dominate you.

Triangulation

Triangulation is when a manipulator invites a third person into your interaction instead of keeping the issue between both of you. For example, a narcissistic partner might involve your parents in a disagreement to get them to take their side. Now, you're suddenly disagreeing with three people and feel overwhelmed.

Manipulators use this tactic to evade personal responsibility or to protect themselves from feeling like they lost an argument.

'Moving the Goalposts'

No matter how much you show up for a manipulator, they constantly change their expectations to keep you trying to reach their 'goalposts.' They do this to frustrate and exhaust you. With narcissists, psychopaths, or Machiavellians, you will never reach the goalposts, regardless of how hard you try. And they will never acknowledge your effort or success if you somehow do.

Apart from these tactics, there are more insidious manipulation tactics, such as gaslighting and love bombing. We will discuss these individually in separate chapters because they are the two main manipulative techniques.

Anyone that can manipulate you can control your thoughts, feelings, and actions. Awareness of the signs and tactics of psychological manipulation is the foundational step to protecting yourself from emotional abuse.

If you're a victim of manipulation, being confused, hurt, and disappointed is normal. Understand that the manipulator's behavior isn't a reflection of you. Manipulation can take a toll on your mental well-being. And it is sometimes subtle enough to go unrecognized for years.

However, often, manipulative people employ the same tactics. Once you know what to look for now, it becomes easier to avoid manipulation in the future.

Quick Reminder
Don't Miss Out to Claim Your Copy Today

SCAN THE QR CODE NOW

CHAPTER 7:
Deception

Deception is characterized by lying, telling half-truths, withholding information, making vague statements, or minimizing facts. It is the act of encouraging people to accept untrue information.

Most people are generally honest, but even honest people engage in deceptive behavior sometimes. According to studies, the average person lies at least twice daily. Some are little white lies ("You look good in that dress") used to spare feelings or navigate an uncomfortable situation. In contrast, others are big lies ("I have flirted with that man!") that can potentially damage a relationship.

Trust is the foundation of all relationships, and deception undermines it. The truth is so fundamental to the human experience that most people assume everyone is truthful in their dealings and communications. Most cultures encourage strong sanctions against lying, a form of deception.

Concealing the truth or deliberately omitting information is considered lying when done to deceive or mislead another person. Additionally, deception includes statements that distort or misrepresent the facts of a situation. It is possible to lie through strategic silence or outright statements.

Some may purposely fabricate false information or stories. But usually, sheer fabrications aren't at the soul of lying. Instead, deception is when someone omits information, denies the truth, or exaggerates information. Or when they agree with others for self-serving reasons.

Deception also happens internally, when people lie to themselves for reasons such as maintaining self-esteem or delusions.

There are many reasons why someone might lie to deceive you. They could be harmless, well-intentioned, or deliberately attempting to inflict pain and suffering. Common reasons for lying include:

- Avoiding embarrassment, conflict, or facing the outcomes of one's behavior.
- Fear of rejection or abandonment.
- Hiding something one did or didn't do.
- Making oneself look good or more talented, unique, and successful than one is.
- Protecting someone else's feelings.
- Maintaining control over a person or situation.

Regardless of the reasons for deception, it can undermine trust and create damage to a relationship.

Studies have long been conducted on how best to detect when a person is lying. Some people, including the dark triad personalities, are more skilled at lying and deception than others. They know how to synchronize their vocal and visual cues with anything they are saying.

Furthermore, it's been proven that most people perform poorly at detecting deception. For some reason, many have unfounded beliefs about indicators of lying – for instance; they consider fidgeting a dead giveaway of lying. This often turns out to be inaccurate.

Some experts argue that "lies are like wishes –" often, people lie compulsively about what they wish was true. People lie for three reasons: to get something they want, to promote or protect themselves, and inflict harm on others. Some people lie to avoid punishment, but this rarely applies to people who use dark psychology tactics.

While everyone sometimes lies, a tiny percentage of people do most of the deceiving and lying. Evidence suggests that skilled liars tend to share the trait of Machiavellianism and Psychopathy.

You might be wondering, "How do I detect deception then?"

As mentioned earlier, it's easy to misinterpret behaviors associated with lying. So, even if you believe a person is lying, you can't always tell for sure. Spotting a lie or deception isn't as simple as observing body language.

Still, the following signs are usually present when someone is lying, being vague, or withholding information:

- Avoiding eye contact
- Providing vague details
- Unusual, body language such as; playing with hair, slouching, rubbing brow, or rigidity.
- Defensiveness when questioned.
- Inconsistencies
- Evasive responses
- Sweat on the brows.
- Offering more information than necessary or more specifics than asked for.
- Smugness
- Stalling
- Repeating "no" many times
- Unusual stillness or calmness

It is possible to mistake distraction, lack of eye contact, or nervousness for deception. Relying only on these signs can lead to mislabeling a person's behavior. Nonverbal cues of lying vary from individual to individual and are hard to detect.

So, let's look at some definitive tell-tale signs of lying and deception.

TELL-TALE SIGNS OF DECEPTION

Here, we will look at research-based signs of deception based on studies from the 1970s. Linguists and psychologists organized controlled experiments where they studied participants' language and word choices and discovered noticeable differences between deceptive and truthful statements.

First, they analyzed the typical characteristics of truthful statements.

Then, they looked for deviations that indicated participants weren't portraying these characteristics. The following is a list of deviations from the norms of truthful statements, which indicate when a person is altering, withholding, or fabricating information or story.

- **Little to no self-reference**

When an individual is telling the truth, they frequently use the "I" pronoun to describe their actions. For example, *"I got home around 7 pm. My phone was on 'do not disturb' so I couldn't hear it ringing. I walked straight to the bathroom. Then, I whipped up a quick meal and settled in to watch my favorite HBO show. It took a while for me to check my phone, which is when I saw your missed calls."* This statement uses the pronoun "I" five times in five sentences.

A deceptive person will use language that minimizes self-references. They might do this by describing the event in the passive voice. For example, *"The phone was on 'DND' so it didn't ring out."*

Another method they use to reduce references to themselves is to use "you" instead of "I." For example, suppose you ask your partner why they got home so late. They might reply, *"Sometimes you get so carried away with work, and time flies. It's easy to lose track of time when you're really busy."*

In face-to-face conversations or text communication, a deceptive person might omit self-referencing pronouns when lying or omitting vital information.

- **Answering questions with questions**

Even the best liars would rather not lie sometimes. Outright lies are easier to detect than fabrications or omissions. Ask a deceptive person a question, and they'll try to evade it with another question before coming up with a fitting lie. They would rather avoid answering at all than lie. But if that doesn't work, they move on to actual lies.

A standard method of evading questions is to respond with a question of their own, such as:

"Why would I cheat on you?"

"Do I seem like the kind of person to do something like that?"

"Don't you think I'd have to be pretty stupid to steal money from my girlfriend?"

- **Use of present tense.**

Usually, when someone tells the truth about something that happened, they use the past tense. Deceptive people subconsciously sometimes describe events as occurring in the present. According to experts, this suggests they're playing it out in their heads.

You should always consider points in a story where the speaker changes from past to present tense usage. Look at the statement below for example:

*"After leaving work, I dropped my phone in the backseat of my car and started driving home. It was raining so I drove slowly. I remembered I wanted to get something at the mall, so I decided to stop on my way. As I pulled into the parking lot, another driver **hits** the car. Thankfully, it caused no damage but there was an argument because he wouldn't take responsibility for being reckless. That's why I was late."*

- **Equivocation**

A deceitful person might evade your questions by filling their statements with weak or vague expressions and modifiers. Watch out for words such as: guess, think, maybe, might, approximately, sort of, could, and about.

These vague expressions of uncertainty allow the individual to deny or alter their assertions another time without outrightly contradicting their original story.

- **Euphemisms**

Most languages have alternate terms for nearly every situation or action. Statements from a deceptive individual will include mild, vague words rather than exact synonyms. Deceptive people employ euphemisms to portray themselves in a more favorable light and reduce any harm their behavior might have caused.

Suppose you suspect your abusive partner is stealing from you and confront them. Naturally, they will lie to conceal the truth. So, watch out for euphemistic words such as "borrowed" in place of "took" or "warned" instead of "threatened."

- **Oaths**

Although someone deceiving you tries to give as vague details as possible, they will try hard to convince you they are telling the truth. They might use oaths to make their stories more convincing. They might sprinkle expressions like "I swear," "Cross my heart," or "On my honor" in their stories. Someone telling the truth doesn't feel the need to back their story with oaths.

HOW TO DETECT DECEPTION

Having established that deception can be hard to detect, you might be wondering if there are things you can do to improve the accuracy of lie detection. The good news is there is a cognitive approach to detecting deception.

This approach emphasizes creating cognitive overload for the person you suspect of lying. A truthful individual conveys the truth with minimal cognitive processing. In contrast, a liar experiences a spike in cognitive processing because they have to recall made-up facts.

Cognitive load is the pressure on the person's attention, memory, and other cognitive processes. For example, environmental distractions such as noise decrease the ability to access the cognitive resources available to someone trying to remember the facts of an event.

Additionally, the liar must control their verbal and nonverbal cues while monitoring their cues to ensure they're absorbing and believing the story. Lying places, a greater demand on a person's mental processes. Therefore, increasing their mental load during the conversation makes it harder to form a lie.

When there is an increased cognitive overload, a liar unknowingly leaks verbal, nonverbal, and language indicators of deception.

In this context, a leakage is anything that cues you to the fact that the person is probably being deceitful. Examples of leakages due to cognitive overload include narrative vagueness, uncertainty, frequent pausing, leaning backward away from you, etc.

The following are four simple techniques to detect deception by increasing cognitive load.

1. Ask the suspected liar to tell the story in reverse.

The first technique involves asking the person to recall the story in reverse order. Liars generally prepare a chronological narrative order for their stories. They start from the beginning and recall facts in chronicle progression.

Once they come up with a believable story, they often practice narrating it multiple times until the facts are memorized, and they can repeat the story without a hint of hesitation or doubt. They rarely practice their lies in reverse orders.

Recalling an event in reverse order can be cognitively taxing. If the event truly happened as narrated, they should have little trouble narrating it in reverse order. However, when an individual is being deceitful, they need increased mental processing to repeat their story backward.

Asking a suspected deception, "Please tell me what happened again but start from the end," puts a greater demand on their mental processing. Consequently, the liar might hesitate, narrate facts out of logical order, or become frustrated. These are irrefutable signs of deception.

2. Encourage them to say more.

Generally, someone telling the truth can quickly offer more

information on request. On the other hand, a liar will have to make up additional details in their head. That makes them susceptible to mistakes and inconsistencies. The extra details you requested might be inconsistent with previously available information or verifiable facts.

3. Ask random questions.

If given enough time, someone who wants to deceive you will prepare by anticipating the questions you may ask. Detecting previously rehearsed lies is much more challenging as they are less likely to be accompanied by typical verbal and nonverbal deception cues.

So, an effective way to detect deception in any situation where the person has had plenty of rehearsal time is to ask unanticipated questions. Unlike someone telling the truth, a liar will find it harder to provide more information or answer your questions quickly and consistently. They might have to take a moment to answer any unexpected question you throw at them.

For instance, a deceptive individual may struggle to accurately describe their emotions during the situation since they didn't experience the event.

At that moment, the liar must take a minute to think about how they would have felt if they experienced what they were relating to you.

Hesitation, answering your question with a question, and using filler words like *um* and *ah* are some tactics they may use to get enough time to come up with an appropriate answer.

4. Maintain eye contact.

The fourth technique is to ask the suspected liar to maintain eye contact with you. This is another tactic to increase their cognitive load. Maintaining eye contact has shown significant differences between a truthful person and a liar in studies about deception.

Asking the liar to maintain eye contact also amplifies the verbal and nonverbal clues of deception, boosting your chances of detecting deception. Many parents use this technique successfully to determine when their kids are lying.

Of course, you have to be cautious when using this technique. Asking people to look you in the eye is considered disrespectful in some cultures, so it may not be a sign of deception for some people.

People with specific medical conditions may avoid eye contact for reasons other than deception. Therefore, you must ultimately employ discernment when using these techniques to recognize deceptive behavior.

The bottom line is that it isn't easy to tell when someone is lying or being deceitful. To identify a liar, you should always look for the signs of deception we discussed earlier. Because deception is cognitively taxing and uses plenty of a person's mental resources, I recommend watching for the signs of deception you learned about only after increasing the liar's cognitive load. That should make it much easier to distinguish someone telling the truth from a liar.

Also, practice regularly in everyday situations to improve your skills and become better at detecting lies and deception. That will prepare you for whenever you meet a master deceiver, such as an individual with any of the dark triad traits.

The next chapter dives deep into one of the major, most destructive manipulation tactics known to man, i.e., gaslighting.

Gaslighting is an insidious manipulation tactic that leaves victims confused and disconsolate as they doubt their sanity. The next chapter will explore the gaslighting phenomenon, its impact, and what you can do about it.

Ultimately, by exposing you to standard gaslighting techniques and equipping you with valuable information, you will be encouraged to break free from the grips of your gaslighter.

CHAPTER 8:
Gaslighting

"Gaslighting provides malignant narcissists with a portal to erase the reality of their victims without a trace. It is a method that enables them to commit covert psychological murder with clean hands."

– Shahida Arabi.

"Gaslighting" originated from the 1938 play *Gaslight* and its 1944 movie adaptation. In the movie, a man deliberately does things to make his wife feel as if she's losing her sanity. He manipulates her perception of reality through various deceptive acts, such as hiding jewels and convincing her she stole them, after which he would place them in her purse.

One of his most notable acts was adjusting the brightness and dimness of their gas-powered house lights while convincing his wife that the changes in the lights were all in her head. He also isolated his wife from family and friends by telling them she was mentally unstable. The gaslighting continued for a period as his wife became increasingly confused to the point where she started questioning her sanity.

Have you ever had someone tell you that you're "losing your mind?" Perhaps by an ex-romantic partner? Maybe you feel something "off" about your current relationship but can't pinpoint it. Perhaps your partner always says things like, "That's not what happened," or "Your memory about that event isn't correct."

While seemingly harmless, these questions often indicate an underlying relationship dynamic that can be severely harmful to one party.

Gaslighting is a term that describes a malevolent power tactic in which a gaslighter tries to induce in their victim a sense that her memories, perceptions, beliefs, and reactions are unfounded in reality – so unfounded that her behavior may qualify as crazy.

A gaslighter deliberately and strategically feeds their victims false information, leading them to question things they know to be true, usually about themselves. Consequently, the victim may doubt their perception, memory, and sanity. Over time, gaslighting can become increasingly complex and powerful, making it harder to see reality as it is.

Gaslighting occurs in all types of interpersonal relationships, although it is more prevalent in intimate relationships. It is the favorite manipulation tactic of narcissists, abusers, and dictators. Their ultimate aim is to gain power and control over someone else by making the person doubt their reality and self-worth, leading them to depend on the abuser for guidance and security.

As a control tactic, gaslighting leaves victims in a foggy state of altered reality. The gaslighter has all the power in the relationship, and they use that to oppress their victim. They often employ another manipulation tactic called triangulation, which involves communicating through third parties rather than directly.

Gaslighting also involves sidestepping evidence that supports the victim's perception of things and labeling them as cognitively impaired. To this end, a gaslighter will use phrases such as *"You're over-sensitive,"* *"You're crazy,"* *"You need help,"* *"Lighten up! It's never that serious,"* and *"I was only kidding."*

Many gaslighting techniques use stereotypes about the victim's sex, race, etc., to attack their vulnerabilities. For example, a common stereotype is that women are sensitive. So, a gaslighting boyfriend might criticize his girlfriend for being "too emotional" when she expresses her feelings about his manipulations. Or he might call her weak for not tolerating his misogynistic jokes.

Some manipulative people use gaslighting to gain control over their victims simply because it gives them a twisted sense of pleasure. In contrast, others do it to control the victim emotionally, sexually, or financially.

ARE YOU BEING GASLIGHTED?

A relationship with a gaslighter starts on a relatively good note. The gaslighter may shower you with praise and compliments on the first date and even confide in you.

Disclosure of an intimate type helps to establish trust before intimacy. It's a vital part of another manipulation tactic called love bombing. The quicker you become enamored with the person, the easier it is to begin the subsequent psychological manipulation and abuse phase.

The gaslighter will begin by lying about simple things and gradually increase the misinformation they feed you daily. They may accuse you of lying if you question their lies and narratives.

This person will use occasional praises and compliments as positive reinforcement to make you unable to predict their moves. But at the same time, they will take steps to turn your family, friends, and other people in your life against you by telling them you're delusional or having memory issues.

Anyone can fall victim to gaslighting techniques, which have been used throughout history by dictators and cult leaders and are still used by people with dark personality traits. The best gaslighters are challenging to identify. You may better recognize them by their victim's mental state and behavior.

Those inclined to employ gaslighting as a tool for psychological abuse are narcissists, psychopaths, and people with specific personality disorders.

If there's one thing we've established in this book, it's that manipulators often present one face to the public and another to their victims privately. Understandably, this makes their victims assume that no one will believe them if they ever speak out or seek help for their abuse. Gaslighters tend to repeat the same behaviors and tactics across different relationships.

How is gaslighting different from manipulation?

Gaslighting is a form of manipulation. However, ordinary manipulation is relatively common, and nearly everyone can manipulate another person to some extent. Gaslighters are rare.

Advertisers create ads to manipulate consumers, and children start manipulating their parents from a young age. But the pattern of abuse involved in gaslighting isn't something that any ordinary person can employ. Those who use this form of manipulation are people who abuse it with the intent to control and dominate other people.

Gaslighting takes different forms and phrases. If you suspect someone is gaslighting you, here are some things they may do to distort your perception and reality.

- They tell outright lies. You know they are lying. Still, they keep a straight face while telling you this lie. Why are they telling it so blatantly? Because they're setting a precedent. Once they tell one huge lie, you can't be sure if anything they tell you is accurate. That keeps you unsteady and off-kilter, which is their actual goal.
- They deny something they said to you, even when you have the proof. Perhaps they promised to do something. They made the promise to your face. But they blatantly deny ever

making the promise. It makes you start doubting your reality – maybe you imagined them saying it. The more this happens, the more you question your reality and start relying on theirs.
- Their actions contradict their words. When dealing with a gaslighter, it's best to focus on what they do rather than what they say. Their words mean nothing; they carry no weight. The real issue is what they are doing. If this person's words never match their actions, that's a red flag.
- They use occasional positive reinforcement to confuse you. One

minute they're telling you that you're worthless and without value and cutting you down; the next, they praise you, saying you're the best thing to ever happen to them. They do this to make you uneasy and unsure of yourself – *"Maybe he isn't so bad after all."* But he is terrible. Pay attention to what they praised you for, and it's most likely something that benefitted them.

- They project their feelings and actions onto you. You know this person is an alcoholic, yet they constantly accuse you of drinking. They do this so often that you become distracted from their behavior and focus on defending yourself against their baseless accusations.
- They try to turn family and mutual friends, and acquaintances against you. Gaslighters are masters at creating an army of people who will stand by them against you. They might say things like, "Sarah thinks you're going crazy too," or "Your mother knows you're worthless." Note that these people may not have said anything like that about you. Gaslighters are pathological liars. They use this tactic to make you feel like you can't trust or turn to anyone – leading you right back to them. Isolation is their goal because it gives them more control over you.
- They tell your loved ones you're crazy or delusional. This is one of the gaslighter's most effective tools. They know if

they plant doubts about your sanity in people's minds, they won't believe you whenever you decide to come out about the abuse. It's a master tactic.
- They convince you everyone else is a liar. By repeating to you that everyone except them is a liar, they make you question your perception again. They couldn't possibly be lying, right? Who would have the audacity to make up false things about others like this? But it's just a manipulation technique to get you to always come to them for the "truth" – which is not true at all.

What about observing signs that may help you recognize if you're being exposed to this form of psychological abuse? Watch out for the following feelings and experiences:

- Constantly doubting yourself.
- Constantly wondering if you're being too unreasonable, sensitive, or unloving.
- Feeling like you are a different person than you used to be.
- Apologizing a lot – even when it's unnecessary.
- Constantly feeling guilty or like you're in the wrong.
- Sensing that something is "off" without knowing what it is.
- Feeling like you can't trust your thoughts or gut.
- Worrying that you aren't "good enough."
- Loss of self-confidence.
- Struggling to make independent decisions.
- Feeling isolated from friends and family.
- Withholding information about your relationship or partner from your loved ones.
- Feelings of hopelessness and helplessness.
- Losing interest in things you ordinarily enjoy.
- Excusing the gaslighter's actions and behaviors, even when you sense they are objectively wrong.

These should give you an idea of whether you're being gaslighted. The more you know them, the easier it is to avoid getting entrapped in the gaslighter's web of manipulation.

HOW TO PROTECT YOURSELF FROM GASLIGHTERS

Gaslighting can leave you confused, betrayed, hurt, and enraged. It's natural to react this way to the realization that an individual you trusted and cared for has been mistreating you and exploiting your vulnerabilities.

But it's important to proceed with caution. One mistake you should never make is expecting your gaslighter to own up to their abusive behavior. Let's look at some techniques that can help you minimize the destructive effects of being gaslighted.

Preemptive Techniques

1. **Train your mind to focus.** The human perceptual system responds differently according to the things we perceive. Your brain automatically screens input and prioritizes the more important ones. Screams, gunfire sounds, the sensation of burning on your skin, sirens, etc., are some things that have been programmed into the nervous system to grab your attention immediately. This is because they signal threats or danger.

   You can train your mind to process new inputs like this. Training yourself to proceed cautiously when making commitments or offering opinions will subsequently make these opportunities in general interactions to set off alarms that call your attention.

   In the short term, you might find it helpful to write down your opinions and expressions of commitments to others for future reference – especially with anyone you suspect to be a gaslighter.

2. **Formalize it.** When you do commit to an opinion or a promise, it helps to make it formal. Ideally, this would mean putting it in writing and having both parties sign it. But this isn't pragmatic in many situations. Under these circumstances, state your perception of your commitment or opinion, then ask the person to confirm that you're correct. Example: "*We agree that you'll pay for our dinner, and I'll help you move into your new home next Friday. Correct?*" Consider writing this down for future reference if you suspect someone might try to gaslight you later.

Transactional Techniques

1. **Ask for multiple details.** If you think someone is trying to convince you of something you know isn't true, ask them to provide multiple details about the event or situation. Anyone trying to gaslight you will likely contradict themselves if you persistently ask for details.
2. **Ask them to verify.** "*I can't recall saying that. Was anyone else present during the conversation?*" For example, let's say a friend tries to gaslight you by asking if they could come to pick up your car later tonight. You tell them you need the car, but they reply that you promised they could have the car for the weekend. However, you don't remember this happening and make it clear to them. They accuse you of going back on your word. In that case, ask them to clarify precisely when you said they could pick up the car. If they can't, you should tell them you don't appreciate them lying and trying to gaslight you.

Apart from these techniques, here are more practical steps to stop gaslighting.

- Become familiar with the signs of gaslight you learn about in this book.

- Listen to your gut feeling. Should you feel like something is "off" about your relationship, don't ignore that feeling.
- Don't second-guess yourself, no matter what. If you believe something to be true, don't let another person discredit you.
- Keep your loved ones close and regularly check in with them. As the gaslighter draws you in, other people's insight can help you see the reality of that situation.
- If someone makes assertions about your mental wellness, do not accept them. Consult your loved ones and a professional if necessary.
- Don't try to one-up the gaslighter. They will seek revenge and won't relent until they get it.
- Don't let the gaslighter know that you're afraid or upset. It'll only reinforce their motivation to get under your skin.
- Get out of the relationship as quickly as possible. Continual exposure to the gaslighter can cause long-term damage if you aren't careful.

The gaslighter's primary goal is to keep you hooked. If you question them, they may make it seem like you're victimizing them. They might try to lure you back with positive reinforcements if you leave.

We call this "hoovering," which may involve the abuser telling you how much they love you and praising your positive qualities. They might promise that things will change between you. But as soon as you go back, things will return to how they were.

Many victims usually end up escaping their gaslighter, leaving the abuser in search of a new person to victimize; often, manipulators already have another target in mind.

CHAPTER 9:
Love-Bombing

Wanting your partner to show their affection is only standard. Little reminders from them demonstrate that you're appreciated and cared for. That can brighten dark days. Displays of affection create security in a romantic relationship, staving off feelings of mistrust, self-doubt, and resentment.

However, what does it mean when displays of love seem overwhelming and overbearing in the early phase of a relationship – to the point where you feel uneasy? Is that still a display of emotion, or is something else at play?

The term "love bombing" was first used by members of the Unification Church of the United States, also called "Moonies" – a religious group commonly considered a cult. In that context, love bombing was used to describe tactics used by the church members to recruit new people, such as excessive flattery and admiration. In the context of a relationship, love bombing takes this same approach.

Love bombing describes the act of bombarding someone (usually an intimate partner) with excessive attention and affection, especially in the form of compliments and gifts. Often, this seems merely like the actions of a newly infatuated lover, but it's a tactic used by manipulators to create a power imbalance in their relationship.

As a manipulation technique, love bombing is commonly associated with narcissists. People with high narcissism love bomb to receive attention, praise, and admiration from others. Their intention isn't to express genuine affection but to obtain control and achieve personal gains.

Displays of affection and attention are expected at the beginning of any romantic relationship but are typically excessive when love bombing is in motion. At first, a new partner may shower you with praise, gifts, and other grand gestures that look like flattery at a glance.

These are manipulative tactics meant to groom you, isolate you from your support system, and establish the abuser as the most important person in your life, ultimately making you emotionally and socially dependent on the love bomber.

As the relationship progresses, the love bomber starts displaying other behaviors, like emotional detachment and coldness. This sets the stage for psychological abuse, including gaslighting.

Love bombing is typically used as a tool for establishing control. It can make you feel ungrateful or guilty if you feel uneasy with your partner's gestures or at odds with them. You might ignore your gut feelings, for example, because you feel obligated to do what they want after everything they've done for you.

When being love-bombed, victims tend to want to do things they ordinarily wouldn't do. For instance, if your partner asks something of you that you don't want to do, you might think, "Well, my partner does so much for me, so I owe this to them, at least."

Not all displays of affection are love bombing. Unlike regular acts of love, love bombing is characteristically immediate and intense and may make the receiver uncomfortable.

The over-the-top display of affection in love bombing isn't just about flowers, vacations, and other romantic gestures. It also invariably includes lots of talks about "our future," how many kids to have together, the ideal dream house for the family, etc.

It's this combination of words and actions that makes love bombing so effective. Considering the ability to text, email, or connect via social media 24/7 which makes it easy to be in nonstop contact with people more than ever, love bombing is more powerful today than it ever was.

This dark psychology tactic is as powerful because of our natural need to feel good about ourselves, and we usually can't fulfill this need independently. Sometimes, an individual's need for external validation is situational, caused by job loss or divorce. Other times, it's ever-present and goes back to the person's childhood.

Whatever the root cause, love bombers are masters at detecting low self-esteem and taking advantage of it.

The irony is that those who love bomb don't exactly go out seeking people who broadcast their insecurity to the world. In contrast, love bombers are also insecure, so they seek out those who they believe would be a great "catch" to feed their own ego.

Perhaps the beautiful woman who appears lonely because men are intimidated by her beauty. Or the successful career guy whose fiancée left for his best friend. Sometimes, it's the badass businesswoman who is averse to marriage and motherhood due to a traumatic childhood.

On paper, these are attractive and seemingly powerful folks, but an incident in their lives makes them doubt their self-worth. Along comes the manipulator with his love-bombing tactic, showering them with attention and affection.

This new romance triggers a dopamine rush that is more powerful than usual. If the victim had a healthy self-perception, it certainly wouldn't be as effective. It works because the manipulator fulfills a need the target can't meet on their own.

Love bombers are emotional vampires – they use affection and attention to establish trust, as a way of asserting control and dominance, and end up draining the joy and emotion right out of their victims. In fact, victims commonly use the word "drained" to describe how they feel in such abusive relationships.

THE LOVE BOMBING CYCLE

The key to discerning the difference between love bombing and romantic courtship is to pay attention to what happens after you enter an official relationship. If your partner continues to display affection so grandly and their actions match words, and you don't feel devalued, then there's probably no love bombing in motion. You might be annoyed by that much attention, but it isn't toxic in and of itself.

On the other hand, if this person abruptly shifts from being affectionate and loving to possessive and controlling while making unreasonable demands, that's your first hint that you're in a cycle of love bombing. It's classic psychological conditioning.

Love bombing serves as the positive reinforcement (I'll shower you with love if you keep doing what I want), whereas devaluation is your negative consequence (I am punishing you because you did something wrong).

The love bombing cycle includes three phases:

- **Idealization:** The first phase involves gifts, compliments, and plenty of attention. The love bomber will be in constant contact with you. They will bombard you with calls, texts, and flowers. They will sweep you off your feet, triggering a nonstop rush of dopamine. They will make early commitments to keep you hooked. You may find this flattering, but that's a sign that they're idealizing the relationship too quickly. Everything in this phase happens too quickly.
- **Devaluation:** Once you start to feel secure with your new partner, they tactically shift from affectionate to critical and controlling. They will devalue you, making you feel as if nobody else would ever want you. This phase often includes threats of abandonment. All of these are a tool for your narcissistic partner to control you.

Usually, relationships in this toxic cycle go through numerous repetitions of the first two phases. Each cycle, the devalued partner works hard to get their abuser's affection back, usually by giving up something they love – such as family, friends, financial power, hobbies, etc.

- **Discard:** In some cases, the love bomber might end the relationship abruptly. This phase happens for one of these reasons. First, the love bomber no longer finds the devalued partner attractive, usually because they've lost the quality that appealed to the abusive partner in the first place.

Second, the victimized partner starts to push back out of frustration, defending boundaries or demanding reciprocity. If the devalued partner shows that they'll no longer tolerate the manipulation and abuse, the love bomber feels exposed and discards the current partner for a new, shiny one who doesn't see beneath the facade yet.

Thirdly, the discard phase is just another part of the manipulation process. Months or years later, the love bomber may come back without warning, promising a new future. Curiously, there will be no apologies for their actions. This return is another attempt at regaining power and control over the discarded lover.

Accepting the love bomber back kick-starts another cycle of abuse.

No matter how the manipulator does it, the final phase always comes as a shock to the devalued partner. Even for victims who push back against their abuser. *How could he do this, especially after everything I sacrificed to make him happy? Weren't we supposed to be together forever?*

SPOTTING LOVE-BOMBING

Spotting a love bomb can be easy, given enough time, but harder in the short term. If a new date sends you flowers after your first date, you should raise an eyebrow. Of course, it could be a mere romantic gesture. But what if it's not?

How do you know if that new person who have you daydreaming and feeling like a teenager is laying the groundwork for psychological abuse?

If the person does any of the following before the six months mark,

it's time to take a step back, slow down, set boundaries, and remind yourself that "If it seems too good to be true, it likely is."

1. "I know we just met, but we are perfect together."

A love bomber will not simply walk up to you and say: "Our future looks perfect." No. They will *show* you that it's true. They will pretend to be a good listener, gathering intelligence on your likes, dislikes, hopes, dreams, and insecurities. Using the intel, they convince you that "we both have so much in common. We must be soul mates!"

Consider your best friend. How much do you have in common? How often do you agree and disagree? Now, think about how long it took to build your bond. Is it possible for someone you met recently to know you as well as your best friend?

That's a litmust test that can get the warning bells ringing.

2. "We have a bright future together!"

Love bombers don't just tell you that you're perfect together; they will describe your future from the minutest details to the biggest one, as though you were both lead actors in a Hollywood romantic movie. *We're going to grow old together. Someday, we will travel the world together. I can't wait for you to meet my family. I want you to have my last name.*

Note that these are all conclusions, not questions or consultations. The love bomber won't ask what you want the future to look like; they simply declare with a strong conviction. Still, they don't come off as crazy or delusional to you, because you've likely shared your dreams and aspirations with them, while they acted as a "good listener." So, they pretend to be the hero of your story who will bring your dreams and hopes alive.

That is how the love bomber manipulates you into thinking they are central to your future happiness.

3. "You deserve the world because you're perfect!"

To delude you into thinking you've met your soul mate, the love bomber idealizes you. They minimize your bad traits and exaggerate the good ones. Tell them you've gained a few pounds and they'll mention that you look so much healthier and radiant with the extra weight.

Did your wife leave you for your best friend? They will make a fuss about how crazy, stupid, and blind she must have been to leave the best man anyone could ever have.

Complain about a supervisor who criticizes you, the love bomber will tell you that he or she must be the biggest idiot on earth for not appreciating your talents.

The love bomber takes every opportunity to build the self-image you're struggling with. They will put you on a pedestal 24/7: Nonstop text sessions, flowers to your workplace, morning notes extolling you; trips, surprise visits, and presents, all with the same slogan: "You deserve the world!"

Ask the following questions to determine if you're being love bombed:

- Is this individual showing an extreme interest in your career, hobbies, and family?
- Does the person praise and criticize you in the same breath – supposedly for your good?

- Do you feel nervous and overwhelmed around the person?

Now, take some minutes to identify if the following red flags have shown up at any point in your relationship. They will alert you to the realization that your partner is likely a skilled manipulator. Here's what to look for specifically:

- They give over-the-top compliments and exaggerated praise. They somehow know what you want to always hear.
- They like huge public displays of affection, both in real life and on social media. Your relationship looks perfect to outsiders.
- They dismiss your needs and ignore your schedule, imposing theirs on you.
- When they make a lavish or grand gesture, they hold it over you. They remind you of the expensive gifts you've received at every chance they get, particularly when you're second-guessing the romance.
- You fear being berated or punished. You feel uneasy around them.
- You constantly must reassure them of your love and commitment. If you don't answer the phone or return a call on time, they become enraged and maybe threaten you.
- They isolate you from your friends and family.

If you fear that you're in the first phase of a love bombing abuse cycle, here's what you must first do:

- **Stop:** Slow down immediately. Sit with the love bomber and tell them: "I love everything about you, but I'm afraid things are moving a little too fast and that scares me. I want us to slow down a bit."
- **Look:** Does this person's words and actions match? If they don't, that's a huge red flag.
- **Listen:** Listen carefully to everything the love bombe says and challenge their assertions. If they say, "We will have a

perfect future together," reply with, "Well, it's still so early, but so far, so good."

Also, keep in mind that love bombers don't like to be challenged. If you challenge an assertion and you get a snarky comment in response, that's another red flag to note.

RECOVERING FROM LOVE BOMBING

On the other hand, if it's a tad too late to recognize and flee from a love bomber, follow these steps for recovery.

- **"No contact" mode**

No contact means exactly that – cutting off all forms of communication between you and the love bomber. Block them on all social media platforms and electronics and leave them a note that clearly states that any attempts to reach you by visiting your home or workplace will be considered harassment. You may need to get a restraining order if necessary.

Manipulators often consider "No" a challenge, pushing them to pursue you even harder until you draw a hard line in the sand. It's best to draw this line upfront. You shouldn't try to stay "friends" with a love bomber – it wouldn't work. Additionally, don't open yourself up to communication.

Otherwise, the love bomber will continue attempting to exploit your vulnerabilities, and the abuse cycle will repeat, again and again.

- **Reconnect with a support system.**

One of the keys to love bombing recovery is reconnecting with a healthy support system consisting of family and friends. The love bomber uses isolation to control you, so none of your loved ones can say, "Hey, look what the h--l is happening in your relationship? Leave him now!"

Loved ones can't tolerate the love bomber, because they see the changes and want your old self back. You will need to apologize for disappearing, but they will understand. Come clean about the abuse and they will be sympathetic.

Imagine something similar happens to a close friend and they told you everything that happened to them – would you encourage them to go back or do everything you can to prevent them from reconciling with their abuser?

- **Remind yourself that love bombing is abuse.**

An important thing to never forget is that love bombing is psychological abuse. Love isn't controlling what your partner does or who they see.

Healthy relationships are built slowly and steadily on a series of actions, not overwhelming words and deeds. Love bombers are skilled at talking, but they lash out when held accountable for the things they say.

It's OK to feel confused and betrayed. Plus, the urge to excuse the love bomber's actions is ever so strong due to how hard they worked to tie your sense of self-worth to their opinions. And that's what perpetuates the cycle of idealization, devaluation, and discard.

To conclude this chapter, I want to say that you can make yourself less of a target for love bombers. It's never right to blame victims of abuse, but you can put some things in place to protect yourself from potential love bombing:

Build a healthy support network. Maintain healthy friendships. Stay in touch with your family. Have a few close friends you're comfortable discussing your dating life with and seek their advice on new partners.

Seek fulfillment in other areas of your life other than romantic relationships. Be vocal about your feelings, needs, and wants in new relationships. And always take things slowly and let them build up naturally.

Finally, don't forget to stop, look, and listen.

CHAPTER 10:
Is Someone Using You?

Have you ever got the feeling that someone in your life cares more about what you can do for them than they do about you? Or that you're being manipulated and exploited for personal benefits? You may not have solid proof, but you feel it – and your gut feeling doesn't lie.

When someone feels "used" by another person, it typically means they've been taken advantage of or violated in some way. In many cases, the person being used doesn't recognize the patterns and signs until long after the abuse has been ongoing for a while. On other occasions, the person recognizes right away that they've been exploited for someone else's gain.

Early relationships (going back to childhood) can affect relationship dynamics in adulthood. For instance, if you were raised in a positive family environment, you may be assertive and less likely to be manipulated.

Here, I'll help you to recognize signs that you're being exploited and suggests ways to put a stop to the manipulation.

Sometimes, it's easy to spot when someone is manipulating you for gains. But it can be harder to detect if the behavior is covert. While everyone has different circumstances, some signs that you're being used may include:

- The person asks for money, favors, and other items. For instance, they might ask you to pay their bills or lend them money.
- They impose on you with zero consideration for your time, availability, or preferences. For instance, they may ask to

- borrow your car without prior notice or move in with you early in a relationship.
- They expect you to cater to their needs without reciprocating sometimes. For example, suppose you go out on a date. In that case, they might wait for you to pick up the tab without offering to pay.
- They exhibit disinterest after you meet their needs. For instance, this person may avoid spending time with you unless they have a need to meet, such as sexual intimacy.
- After an initial love-bombing phase, they only show affection and intimacy at their convenience. For instance, they may shower you with affection up until the moment they get what they want.
- They are never there for you when you need them. For example, although they moved into your home, they might decline to give you a ride to work.

Signs you're being used vary depending on the relationship dynamic. If the user is a friend, they may only want to do things together when it is convenient for them. Or expect you to listen to their feelings and needs, but never acknowledge or listen to what you have to say.

If the user is a romantic partner, they may exhibit self-centeredness and disinterest in your needs. Sometimes, it involves a lover only wanting a sexual relationship while declining to make an emotional commitment of any kind.

Being taken advantage of doesn't feel good for victims. Not only can it cultivate a negative self-image but can also negatively impact your future relationships – making it harder to trust new people.

Here are two ways being used might affect you:
- **Mental health:** Being manipulated and exploited can cause significant mental health problems. This may be even worse if you were abused in a previous relationship. It can

trigger symptoms associated with anxiety, trauma, and depression. Over time, you may have difficulty forming new bonds.
- **Relationships:** Being used is a sign of a dysfunctional relationship. It indicates that one person is making sacrifices, whereas the other is taking excessively. It causes a power imbalance within the relationship. Healthy relationships comprise two partners providing mutual trust, support, and emotional security to each other.

Being exploited isn't a good feeling and can lead to mental health issues and relationship-related issues. It helps to be aware of signs that someone may be using you. Even if this person isn't a dark psychology practitioner, it can set a precedent for sniffing narcissists, psychopaths, Machiavellians, and other master manipulators from a distance before they do any damage to you.

ARE YOU VULNERABLE TO DARK PSYCHOLOGY AND MANIPULATION?

Some people are magnets for the dark triad personalities and other practitioners of dark psychology secrets. They end one toxic relationship with a narcissist only to end up with a high Mach. Or maybe they continue to tolerate manipulative behavior from family members or coworkers.

If you relate to this, you are not alone.

You may have asked yourself, *"Is something wrong with me that makes me susceptible to exploitation and manipulation?"* The answer is No, but it's also yes.

Nothing is wrong with you in the real sense of the word, but there's a good chance you exhibit qualities that attract narcissists and manipulators to you, like ants to sugar or moths to a flame. In fact, these might be some of your best qualities. Toxic people recognize this and that's why they employ dark psychology tactics to exploit your good nature for personal gain.

In an earlier chapter, I mentioned that individuals with the dark trade traits lack affective empathy, but are capable of cognitive empathy. The former is the kind of empathy that comes with compassion, whereas the latter doesn't exist with affective traits such as compassion.

Dark psychology practitioners use cognitive empathy to observe,

understand, and control their victims – causing them unspeakable pain and trauma. They lack components of empathy such as compassion, humanity, and remorse.

Using cognitive empathy, manipulators are able to seek out targets that are loving, empathetic, and highly compassionate. These positive qualities give abusers a foot in the door to execute their manipulation tactics and drain the life of their victims.

Many people won't put up with gaslighting, love bombing, and other abusive tactics beyond an early point in a relationship. However, people with empathic qualities fall prey because of their inclination to help, heal, and fix broken people.

With traits like that, one might as well wear a red bullseye for manipulators. But you don't have to put up with manipulating, and you shouldn't. The first step to protecting yourself from manipulation and psychological abuse is identifying the qualities that draw dark psychology practitioners to you in the first place.

- **You're trusting.**

Some believe trust must be earned after meeting someone new. After all, who trusts someone they've just met?

For trusting people, trust is established from the get-go; because you believe everyone is well-intentioned like you. You immediately trust people to be respectful and to do the right thing. Why? You're a trustworthy person yourself – someone with integrity. You expect that people are deserving of trust until they break it.

Narcissists know and use this to their advantage. They know they can get away with deception and lies because you *really want to* trust them. Being naturally trusting makes it easy to ignore obvious red flags in other people.

- **You're a people-pleaser.**

People-pleasing is another quality that can attract narcissists and manipulators to you. It makes you vulnerable to exploitation as you seek to do what would improve others' perception of you or make them like you.

A people-pleaser may view their perceived bond with the manipulator as special and important and, as such, not want to jeopardize their connection.

Individuals with dark triad traits know that people-pleasers depend on attention and affection and fully use that knowledge to their advantage.

- **You have a victim mindset.**

Manipulators typically latch onto people with a victim mindset, usually feeding into that mentality to create the power imbalance needed to coercively persuade you into doing what they want.

For example, let's say you had a fight with a close friend about something. A master manipulator might encourage you to act on that anger and frustration to cut the friend off. This is just another attempt at isolating you from a healthy support network.

- **You struggle with setting and enforcing boundaries.**

Anyone who struggles with setting boundaries is an easy target for narcissists and abusers. This is one of the first things these toxic people look for in a potential victim. People who are good at setting boundaries are equally good at enforcing them upon meeting someone new.

Manipulators are drawn to highly empathetic people who struggle with boundary-setting because they know you will put up with their antics for as long as possible. And by the time you think about setting any boundaries, it's already too late. The abuser will simply mock you, gaslight you, and tear the boundary down.

- **You've experienced abuse or trauma in the past.**

Manipulators are like bloodhounds. They can sniff vulnerabilities from a distance. They have a "spidey" sense for identifying victims who have been abused or exploited in the past. This is why you should never share too many details about yourself with someone you've just met.

Highly manipulative individuals will disguise questions about your past in the form of curiosity. In reality, they are tiring to determine how broken you are and how easy it will be to exploit your vulnerability.

If you can relate to any of the points above, chances are you've been a victim of narcissistic abuse in the past or are currently in an abuse cycle with a parent, friend, coworker, or romantic partner.

The unfortunate thing about manipulation is that it mostly happens in a relationship where the other person knows you in and out. People in close relationships are more vulnerable to manipulation because both parties know their desires, needs, vulnerabilities, and weaknesses.

Still, you cannot distance yourself simply because you fear being used and taken advantage of. So what do you do?

Your best is to master techniques to decrease your susceptibility and increase your cognitive immunity to dark psychology and manipulation tactics. We will deep-dive into this in Chapter Thirteen. But here's a good place to start.

Begin by answering the following questions. I recommend writing them down in a journal so you can review and evaluate your answers for later reference.

- "Do I have an excessive need to please other people?"
- "Am I usually worried about upsetting people?"
- "Is there someone in my life I do certain things for to avoid annoying or making them angry?
- "Do I find it hard to say no? Or do I find myself saying yes even when I want to say no?"
- "Am I always putting a positive spin on people's bad behavior toward me? Do I justify or rationalize their actions?"
- "Do I feel like I have no choice but to remain in my current relationship?"
- "Do I stay in relationships even when they are hurting me?"

If you answered yes to some, most, or all the questions, you're highly vulnerable to manipulation.

Now, it's time to do something about your susceptibility to dark psychology predators. There are many things you can do, but let's start with learning how to decode the body language clues of manipulators, narcissists, and others with dark personality traits.

Knowing how to read and analyze people's body language makes it significantly easier to spot manipulators in your first few meetings. That way, you don't have to make them a part of your life before cutting them off instantly.

Find out body language secrets and tips in the next chapter.

CHAPTER 11:
Decoding Body Language Clues

Body language is a critical component of communication. As I once heard a psychologist say, it is a silent orchestra. It can tell you more about a person than their words. An individual's body language is a subconscious communication of their internal state.

Everyone has specific negative and positive body language habits that they've cultivated over time. Since a person's body language represents their true feelings and conveys their own message in an interaction, it is crucial to have a good grasp on how to decode body language clues.

The goal is to use your mastery of body language to determine if a person's words match their true feelings in any interpersonal interactions.

From the FBI to media commentators and human resource professionals, everyone examines people's body language for clues about their character. You may be familiar with how media commentators scrutinize public figures' facial expressions, postures, and gestures for insight into their beliefs, attitudes, and inner world.

An engineer turned nonverbal communication researcher, Albert Mehrabian, discovered what we now know as the 7-38-55 rule. According to the rule, 7% of all communication is words only (verbal), 38% is a tone of voice, intonation, and other sounds (vocal), and 55% is nonverbal (body language).

Nonverbal communication is so important that industry leaders across different fields hire body language experts to train them to communicate effectively without words.

As an average person going about your day, much of how you perceive body language is subconscious and automatic. For example, someone smiles at you and you may assume a connection. You tell

your boss something and their nod indicates that they understand.

Yet, to truly understand how people, knowingly or unknowingly, communicate nonverbally, you need to learn the secrets of body language. By secrets, I don't mean some hidden knowledge that is only accessible by a privileged few. Rather, I'm talking about things that ordinary, everyday people don't know.

One of the things that make people susceptible to dark psychology tactics is that they don't know how to read people's body language. As a result, they simply take manipulators' words for it. If you've made this mistake in the past, you don't want to repeat it. And if you haven't, you want to ensure things continue this way.

What is body language?

At a basic level, body language is the physical representation of our emotional state. It is the signals our bodies send out to convey our thoughts and feelings to people. Facial expressions, body movements, tone and volume of voice, and other nonverbal signals are collectively referred to as body language.

Microexpressions (quick emotional displays on the face), posture, and hand gestures all register in the brain almost instantly – even when you aren't consciously aware you've perceived something.

Due to this, body language strongly shapes how you are perceived, and how you, in turn, interpret other people's moods, openness, and motivations. It's normal to mirror body language; beginning as early as infancy, newborns start moving their bodies to the rhythm of their primary caregiver's voice.

Decoding means being able to read and analyze these signals. It involves interpreting hidden information, emotions, personality, and intentions from a person's nonverbal communication.

On the other hand, encoding is how you send cues to people you're communicating with. It's how you influence the kind of impression you give, and how they feel when they are around you.

Most of our nonverbal communication happens below the conscious awareness level. For example, suppose you're on a first date with a long-term crush. In that case, you may tap your foot nervously without being aware of the body movement. Similarly, if you arrive at a blind date, you may subconsciously pick up your date's averted gaze or crossed arms, which indicates being closed off.

The good news is, with knowledge and regular practice, you can become skilled at controlling your body language and reading others.

Narcissists and other types of manipulative people are great at encoding and sending the exact body language cues they want. But it's very hard to deceive your subconscious.

So, even if a manipulator tries hard to align their body language with their verbal communication, you can decipher their real feelings and intentions. Often, the giveaway is in how hard they try to come off to you in a certain way.

During my research phase for this book, I came across all kinds of myths. Many of the books I read claimed there were specific body movements all manipulators use. Some claimed that if a person constantly looks to their left during your conversation, that's a sign of deception. I remember reading that manipulative individuals rub their noses in a certain style. I'm afraid none of these are entirely correct.

The simple truth is that mastering body language as a tool for identifying manipulation takes time and practice. If you are serious about learning to detect deception, you must first master the manipulator's body language. Deviations from the standard indicate that something is off with them.

As a result, you may find it easier to spot manipulation when it's from someone you've known for a long time. You're familiar with their normal body language, so it's easier to notice any deviations, whether deliberate or not.

Note that it can be true that someone rubbing their nose or looking to

the left could indicate deception. But this is only true if that gesture is out of the ordinary for the person.

When it comes to skilled manipulators, they have a set of body language clues that they deliberately use to elicit certain emotions in their targets. If you meet a new person and you suspect them of being manipulative, these clues can be strong indicators.

Here are examples of body language clues that a manipulator could use to persuade or covertly influence you.

- **Tilting their head.**

When you feel safe in someone's company, you subconsciously tilt your head. Notice how often everyone tilts their heads the next time you hang out with friends. This body language clue is part of the limbic brain response.

A head tilt exposes the neck and, consequently, the jugular vein. That gesture communicates vulnerability, which subconsciously signals trust and respect. Tilting your head in the company of those you care about conveys comfort and ease.

When a manipulator wants to subtly influence you, they know you're more likely to be susceptible if you feel safe. So, they might do a head tilt to demonstrate attentiveness and listening. That way, you believe they're interested in what you have to say and not just thinking about other things.

Additionally, a person with a tilted head is perceived as having less of an agenda – but that's not true for manipulators.

- **Mirroring your body language.**

Praxis is a phenomenon where two people in a conversation replicate each other's body language. This usually happens subconsciously and indicates that both parties are positively engaged in the conversation.

If someone wants to influence or persuade you, they might mirror your body language to establish rapport. Salespeople commonly use this technique with clients by listening, observing, and mimicking their nonverbal cues, with successful results.

Additionally, someone who is attracted to you will indeed copy your physical movements and mannerisms. Someone looking to manipulate you might replicate your gestures and movements to seduce and get your attention.

It can help to watch out to see if the person you're just getting to know constantly mirrors your body language.

- **Rubbing their neck and hand.**

Visualize your favorite movie villain. Chances are you can easily imagine a scene where they rubbed their hands together or rubbed their neck before or after doing something evil. Even movie producers recognize that this body language typically represents self-serving scheming. Someone with a Machiavellian personality might constantly exhibit this nonverbal clue.

Meanwhile, we rub our necks when we feel stressed or overwhelmed. The best manipulators try not to let their victims know when they're overwhelmed. However, it's impossible to completely hide it.

Suppose you suspect someone is lying to you. In that case, use the cognitive overload technique and then watch if they'll rub their neck. Increasing mental load causes a sort of pressure that the manipulator is bound to feel physically. As a result, they may touch or stroke their neck to pacify themselves.

Notice if they like to rub their neck at the back, sides, and below the chin when narrating a story, you suspect to be false or inaccurate.

- **Constant eye movement.**

There's a common misconception that direct eye contact for a long time implies someone is being truthful. But manipulators are generally good at holding eye contact for as long as necessary. They have rehearsed so many times and become exceptional at it.

As a matter of fact, manipulators constantly watch their victims and look them in the eyes to determine if they're falling for the manipulator's ploy. If someone makes a point of always looking you in the eyes, then you might want to be wary of them.

One more thing to pay attention to is the rate of blinking. It can reveal what's happening to a person neurologically. Increased blinking may point to rising stress, fear, or adrenaline. For manipulators, it's most likely the latter.

Depending on the situation, reduced blinking may mean the person is focused or relaxed. Use your discernment of the context to determine which it is.

- **Shifting body positions.**

Pay attention to how often someone shifts their attention if you sense they're trying to influence or control you. Manipulators may shift their positions to indicate discomfort. They do this because the human mind is innately trained to recognize discomfort and we're wired to offer consolation when we sense that.

Therefore, a manipulative person might continually shift their body positions to get you to cave into an unreasonable demand or request.

- **Always smiling.**

Smiling is a powerful nonverbal cue for portraying charisma. Emotions are infectious. An emotion like happiness can be easily transferred from one person to another via a bright smile. Think about it: you can't bring yourself to frown at a smiling face.

When someone smiles at you, the brain releases neurotransmitters associated with increased happiness and decreased anxiety. Therefore, someone smiling at you can improve your mood. If you smile back, that can boost the person's charisma, helping them to feel more confident and positive about your interaction.

A manipulator can take advantage of that by constantly smiling at you in the early phase of your interactions. Then, you subconsciously start to attribute positive experiences and conversations with them. Unknown to you, they are building likeability and trust, making you want to spend more time around them. It also makes you susceptible to covert influence.

These attributes make the manipulator more persuasive and powerful in your relationship. It's best not to underestimate the power of a smile.

- **Pointing feet.**

I have found it fascinating to observe the direction of my loved ones' feet in social situations ever since I discovered the meaning behind it. The direction your feet point to is considered a sign of where your mind is focused. If a person's feet are pointed at you on a date, that's a good sign that they're engaged in the conversation and are truly listening to you.

On the contrary, if their feet are pointed away from you, that means they are not truly interested in the conversation and are close to exiting.

Pay attention to this whenever you're talking to someone you believe to be a manipulator. If they're talking about how much they want a future with you while their feet are pointed in a different direction, that could be a sign of pretense.

Ultimately, nonverbal cues precede and sometimes override conscious thought; therefore, body language can reveal a person's true feelings – but only if you're aware of the meanings of the gestures, movements, and microexpressions.

Observe closely and a manipulator's thoughts, emotions, and intentions could be laid bare to your discerning eyes – preventing you from falling prey to the predator!

CHAPTER 12:
How to Protect Yourself

Picture this. It's the Friday of a tough week, and you can't wait to get home to spend the evening with your family. Out of nowhere, your boss comes up to you, sits down in your chair, and sighs. "The day sure flew by," she says. "My parents are visiting, but it looks like I might have to stay till late evening to finish a report I was working on. Such a shame because I wanted to spend the evening with them. I rarely see them these days."

"That's sad," you say, now feeling uncomfortable.

Your boss proceeds, "Oh, I actually just remembered that you've handled the report before and got it done in a couple of hours." Then, she leans closer and says, "That also reminds me, I'm meeting with HR in a few days to discuss the idea of you getting a pay raise."

Understandably, you offer to work on the report for her.

In this scenario, you've clearly been manipulated. Unfortunately, it's much harder to protect yourself from this subtle form of passive-aggressive manipulation.

Being a victim of manipulation and dark psychology can be emotionally exhausting and detrimental to your health, especially if repetitive. So, you must learn to protect yourself from covert manipulators like your boss in the above scenario and other people who may try to use dark psychology tactics to take advantage of you.

In this chapter, we'll be discussing three critical steps anyone who wants to protect themselves from manipulation must master.

- Building self-awareness
- Setting limits with manipulators
- Becoming assertive

It can be easy to become upset, angry, hurt, or defensive when you've been manipulated, especially if it's been happening for a long time. Learning to tune in with your emotions, set boundaries, and communicate assertively can help you manage the situation powerfully and effectively.

When you take a stand against manipulators, they might try to use diversionary strategies to confuse you, throw you off-track, or weaken your resolve. Do not let them sidestep or distract you. Instead, focus on these three steps and the issue you wish to address.

Now, let's get to discussing each of these steps one by one.

INCREASE SELF-AWARENESS

In the words of the Chinese philosopher, Lao-Tzu, "It is wisdom to know others; it is enlightenment to know oneself."

Have you ever met a self-aware person? If you have, then you know self-awareness is one of the best qualities that anyone can possess. Building self-awareness is essential in your personal and professional life. Apart from the numerous science-backed benefits, increasing self-awareness can be the first step to protecting yourself against psychological manipulation and abuse.

The first mainstream theory of self-awareness was published in the early 1970s by psychologists Shelley Duval and Robert Wicklund. According to them, self-awareness is "the ability to look inward, think deeply about your behavior, and reflect on how it aligns with your values and moral standards."

When your actions and behaviors don't align with your beliefs and values, you feel distressed, uncomfortable, and unhappy. By contrast, an alignment of your behavior and values makes you feel self-confident and positive.

Self-awareness gives you a deep insight into your opinions, attitudes, and knowledge. It is often confused with self-consciousness, which is a state of hyper-sensitized self-awareness. Self-consciousness is a preoccupation with your appearance, behavior, and mannerisms.

You probably don't know this, but self-awareness is a fundamental component of emotional intelligence. It empowers you with the ability to understand and control your emotions and behaviors. You can already see how that can make you less susceptible to manipulation tactics.

Being self-aware is the single, most effective way to protect yourself from psychological abuse. If you are self-aware, you will know when you're doing what another person wants, rather than what you want.

Manipulation and exploitation often elicit subtle feelings of discomfort. Feeling vaguely disconnected, unsettled, uncomfortable, and imbalanced are all signals your body sends to convey one message: "You're allowing yourself to be manipulated!"

Similarly, growing irritation, frustration, and annoyance – all varying levels of anger – can serve as physiological signs. If you feel like your life is out of order, something is amiss, or you're unfit, these are all warning signs too.

These bodily feedbacks are important signals that you're likely being taken advantage of, whether you realize it on a conscious level or not. Developing "an inner meter on manipulation" through self-awareness is a crucial life skill for setting limits and becoming assertive so that you can stand up for yourself against abusers, gaslighters, love bombers, and other types of manipulators.

Below are four core signs that call your attention to manipulation:

1. **Experiencing discomfort.** You feel uncertain; question the realness of your interpersonal interactions; and feel out of sorts with yourself.
2. **Feeling drained and exhausted after every interaction.** Being with toxic and vile people can make you feel emotionally and physically drained. Psychologists liken this to being around "energy or emotional vampires." You feel drained of feelings, energy, and fortitude.
3. **Value dissonance.** Your actions and words no longer reflect your values and beliefs. This indicates a lack of connection and resonance with your established values system. It means you're now acting in line with someone else's values.
4. **You feel the urge to speak and behave in ways that don't reflect who you are.** You no longer recognize yourself because you're doing things you ordinarily wouldn't do. In other words, you feel out of place with yourself.

The critical factor in these signals is that you're out of sync with yourself. Whenever you start to notice any of these signals, that's a call to examine your inner manipulation meter. These things are easier to notice in people you are close to.

The first step to protecting yourself against manipulation is straightforward: become increasingly self-aware, tune into your feelings and body, and learn to identify when you feel unlike yourself. Most importantly, address it immediately.

So, how do you increase self-awareness?

There are several steps involved in building self-awareness. Keep in mind that it will take time and effort. Once you start building self-awareness, it enables you to take a confident approach to people and situations you find yourself in. In turn, that gives you control of your own life, experiences, and direction.

Here's how you can build and increase self-awareness.

- **Know your strengths and limitations.**

Learning the areas of your life where you're strongest and those where you're limited is a great point to begin building self-awareness. It's difficult for someone who is keenly aware of their strengths and good qualities to be taken advantage of. Also, when you know your limitations (or weaknesses), it's harder for a manipulator to use them against you.

You may also speak to friends and family for clarification on your strengths and limitations. Although many of us believe we're self-aware, external feedback from people who care about us can help us attain a clearer understanding.

- **Start a thought diary.**

A thought diary is an excellent place to start for someone wanting to build awareness. It can be helpful in keeping track of thoughts that pop up automatically, particularly when you're around the manipulator.

Track what was occurring at the time the thought popped up. Mentally note your level of emotional reaction to the event. Once you've recorded the experience in your thought diary, take a few minutes to analyze the underlying feeling experienced at that moment.

Even if you don't have the time to analyze, recording events, thoughts, and feelings in your diary enables you to track recurring patterns. When there's an obvious pattern repeating in every interaction with a particular person, recognizing signs of manipulation or exploitation is easier.

Humans tend to introspect with a self-serving bias, instead of objectively analyzing events and situations to abstractly learn more. So, to ensure efficacy, make the thought diary a fact-finding mission, rather than an emotional exercise.

In other words, leave your personal judgment and feelings aside when analyzing the content of your thought diary.

- **Write a regret letter.**

If you've experienced past trauma, writing a regret letter can help you practice radical forgiveness and increase self-awareness. Address the letter to your former self about present regrets and forgive yourself for mistakes made in the past. Permit yourself to be human.

Finally, consider journaling as a healthy outlet for your feelings and thoughts. You don't have to be a writer to try this strategy. Honesty is at the heart of self-awareness and journaling allows you to be honest with yourself. Permitting yourself to recognize and refocus self-serving bias via journaling is the best decision you can make.

Journaling will offer insight into changes to make and track through your personal experience. You may find it helpful to keep a different journal for different aspects of your life, including career, family, relationships, etc.

By building your self-awareness, you get to know what's acceptable to you and what isn't, and you learn to use that information to set and enforce limits with manipulators.

ESTABLISH AND MAINTAIN BOUNDARIES

Everyone needs personal space and boundaries – time alone to recharge our social batteries, time with family to feel cared for and supported, and time with friends to let loose. Sadly, toxic, manipulative, and abusive people constantly disrespect this need. They violate our personal boundaries, leaving us physically and emotionally drained.

Setting boundaries with your manipulator opens your eyes to just how rampant their malicious behaviors are. When you see how they disrespect your boundaries repeatedly, without care for your feelings, you become tired of the dynamic.

The more the psychological abuse becomes obvious, the higher the chance that you'll finally up and leave the relationship.

Your personal boundaries, also known as limits, are rules that you set to protect yourself physically, emotionally, and mentally – with consequences in place for when they're flouted. Consequences for violation of your personal boundaries are not punishments. Instead, they are about doing something that makes you feel good immediately after the boundary is crossed.

Additionally, personal boundaries can be standards you set for yourself for all interactions and relationships going forward.

Setting boundaries begins with clarifying what your boundaries entail. If you don't know where to begin, the following questions can help you get started.

- What makes me feel uncomfortable?
- What makes me feel disrespected?
- What makes me feel used or taken advantage of?
- What makes me feel unappreciated?

Answering these questions can help you to understand your needs and provide a starting point for establishing personal boundaries. If anyone in your life isn't respecting set boundaries despite many corrections, then you may need to reevaluate your relationship.

Here are some examples of boundaries to set in a relationship:

- Direct or indirect name-calling will not be tolerated, especially where it can be overheard by you or anyone else.
- No subtle abuse implies that you're worthless for having a different opinion than the other person.
- No mind games, word games, technicalities, or rephrasing of your words to derive a different meaning than you originally communicated.

- No attempts to correct your words or dictate the tone in which you should speak.
- No abuse disguised as humor.

Then, you must set consequences for people who violate the above boundaries. Example:

"If someone crosses this boundary and I feel safe communicating with them at that moment, I will tell them, "I feel threatened by your words and tone. I am leaving your presence now to collect my thoughts. Maybe we can connect again later, but I'm doubtful when that will be."

"If I feel unsafe saying something to the person who violated my

boundaries, I will only carry out the consequence and not explain to them. I will leave the environment for as long as it takes until I feel safe to return – if I consider it safe to return."

Do not make excuses for the person violating your boundaries. It's easy to tell yourself that they're having a hard time, or they didn't mean to cross the line. But doing this will only embolden someone who already doesn't care for you or your personal limits. Learn to hold abusive people accountable for their actions and stop letting them off the hook.

The first time you set a boundary for the manipulator in your life, you may feel guilty. It may feel as though taking that step to protect yourself is a crime. The internalized belief that you should be and do just as the person wants is the source of that guilt.

But if you acknowledge how you feel and continue to set necessary boundaries, that guilt will disappear in time. The more you keep track of the things they say and do, the more you will realize how wrong that person is. You will know that they should be the ones feeling bad over their behavior and actions (although they won't).

Writing down your boundaries and keeping a thought diary can help you recognize when the abuse starts. It can make it easier to circumvent the abuse as soon as it begins rather than wait until they turn you into a shadow of yourself.

Setting boundaries will give you a sense of personal strength and responsibility to yourself to stop accepting toxicity so willingly. You will start seeing yourself as an agent of change not just for yourself, but for the relationship as well.

Whether the manipulator is a friend, family member, co-worker, or boss, dealing with them can be challenging – especially when you love and care about them. However, it's important to make a choice in how you let others treat you. You don't have to tolerate their toxic and negative behavior.

By setting boundaries, you can begin to protect yourself from further

exploitation and harm and begin to heal your wounds while setting the tone of how you would like to be treated going forward.

Remember that you have every right to protect yourself from the manipulator's vicious words and malevolent actions.

LEARN ASSERTIVENESS

If you often feel as though people undermine your opinions and views (which is one thing manipulators always do), it could be because you lack the confidence to stand up for yourself. You might feel like you can't do anything about it at the moment, but the truth is that you can.

By learning to become more assertive, you can speak up and confidently maintain your boundaries with manipulators and other people who seek to take advantage of you.

Assertiveness is a skill to better manage yourself, others, and the situations you find yourself in. It can help to influence agreement or behavior change in other people. It involves expressing yourself confidently and positively.

Assertive people are the boss of themselves and know how to be honest with themselves and other people. Before we go any further, I want to note that once you start becoming assertive with your abuser, they will get distressed and eventually leave the relationship as long as you don't back down.

I consider that a win-win situation; not only do you gain control over yourself and your decisions, but you also get rid of toxic people from your life.

Being assertive enables you to find a balance between communicating your own feelings, needs, and wants while respecting those of others. It can be especially helpful if the toxic person in your life is a Machiavellian personality since it makes creating win-win solutions much easier.

Learning to be assertive is about more than just speaking your truth. To be assertive, you must be in tune with your feelings, wants, and needs and know how to manage your positive and negative feelings.

Many assume that assertiveness involves saying what you think or feel, period. But it's not as simple as that.

Assertiveness exists on a continuum: on one end, you come off as weak and the abuser doesn't take you seriously, and on the other end, you come off too strong and the person becomes defensive. That can enrage them to increase the viciousness of their attacks on you. Assertiveness is somewhere around the middle.

You need skill and practice to learn assertiveness. It doesn't come easily to most. And those who find it easy are rarely vulnerable to manipulation and dark psychology tactics. The best way to develop assertiveness is to begin staying attuned to your feelings and needs and taking them seriously.

If you learn to do this, it becomes harder to tolerate people who won't respect or fulfill those needs.

Five assertiveness skills

1. Awareness of your feelings in the present moment.

Being aware of your feelings before and after a situation is helpful, but assertiveness requires being able to identify your feelings in the middle of an encounter.

2. Accept and validate your feelings.

If you feel anger rising in the middle of an encounter with a manipulative partner, know and trust that the feeling is valid. And you deserve to be heard by this person responsible for the feeling.

3. Vocalize your feelings.

This requires you to first identify and validate your feeling within yourself. That way, you're better able to put how you feel into words and express yourself in clear terms to the other party.

4. Try to understand the other party.

You don't want to become like the manipulator, so it is important that you consider their feelings when addressing them.

5. Consider the situation, context, setting, and environment.

Always take some time to determine how best to convey your message. Once you consider the situation, context, and other factors, it will be easier to express yourself in a healthy way to ensure the other person hears you – or at least pretends to.

The following are tips to help you become more assertive:

- **Use "I" statements.** This helps you to communicate what you think or feel without putting the other person on the defensive. For example, say "I disagree," instead of "You're wrong." If you want something from them, say, "I would like you to help with this," instead of, "You should do this." Keep requests specific and clear.

- **Say "no" more often.** If you find it hard to turn down requests and demands, practice saying "no" more regularly. Say, "No, I can't help you with that now." Remember that "No" is a complete sentence. You shouldn't have to explain yourself to the manipulator. Be direct and never hesitate when you say "no." If you need to include an explanation, keep it brief and simple. Don't justify your decision to say no.
- **Rehearse ahead.** If expressing your thoughts and feelings are challenging, practice different scenarios you may encounter with manipulative people. Say your opinion aloud. You can even write it down first and use the script to practice. It might help to role-play with yourself in front of a mirror or with a close friend. Then, ask them for feedback on how to improve.
- **Utilize body language.** You know that a great deal of communication is nonverbal, so use that to your advantage. Act confident even if you don't feel like that. Maintain an upright posture. Look the person directly in the eye and keep a neutral facial expression. Do not cross your arms. Use your words, facial expressions, and body language to convey your message.
- **Manage your emotions.** Acting emotionally when communicating with manipulative people puts you at risk of that emotion being exploited. It's best to keep any emotions in check and don't show them to your abuser – unless it's an emotion that makes you seem strong. But if you feel anxious, fearful, or ashamed of going into a difficult situation, wait a

bit. Then, work on inducing calm and getting your voice to be steady and firm.

Remember, learning assertiveness takes plenty of time and practice. So, don't expect to become assertive as soon as you start practicing. If you don't make progress despite the effort, you should consider signing up for formal assertiveness training. It'll be worth it

CHAPTER 13:
7 Rules of Influence and Power

Power is the ability to make others behave in a desired way based on authority. It involves imposing your will on them, whether they want to or not. If you hold power over people, you can demand that they behave a specific way or commit certain actions.

Even if they don't think you are right or share your beliefs, they will perform the actions because they believe refusing could lead to consequences or rewards that you can enact using your power and authority.

On the other hand, influence is the ability to change a person's behavior based on persuasion rather than authority. Unlike power, influence doesn't involve making demands or simply telling people what to do. Instead, you persuade them into changing how they think, feel, or act using interpersonal skills.

The kind of relationship you have with people determines how influential you are in their lives. When you have a positive relationship built on mutual trust, your actions and behavior will likely influence people naturally.

Both power and influence are tools for changing others' actions and behaviors. However, they both involve significantly different approaches.

Power involves the use of coercion – direct or indirect, whereas influence involves the use of persuasive skills. Influence doesn't rule with an iron fist. Rather, it gently but firmly guides the person through the decision-making process.

Manipulative people seek to gain power over you because they know coercion is the only way they can get you to do the things they want. When you do something, they want, you feel as if you're acting against your values and beliefs, solely because you have to.

If you want to be able to get people to do what you want without using manipulation tactics, then you must combine influence and power. In life, there will always be periods when you'll need power or influence over the other. And in many situations, one method will be more effective than the other.

You shouldn't rely solely on power because influence lasts longer and the effects linger even when you no longer have power. Also, having influence means you don't have to fear losing power.

Power may work effectively in the short term, but the influence is a lasting and more positive motivator to get what you want.

Here are the 7 rules of influence and power.

1. Always build trust and be consistent.

One mistake people make is thinking that influence is periodic. Robert Cialdini, the author of *Psychology of Persuasion* emphasizes that it's impossible to demonstrate integrity in the process of persuasion.

You must establish trust and consistently show people that you have their best interests at heart. To do this, you should build a healthy rapport and show genuine concern for people before any attempt at steering them toward a desired outcome.

To demonstrate trustworthiness, you must be authentic. Find what makes you truly unique and use that to positively impact others. People crave stability, so consistency is vital. Contradictions make you come off as untrustworthy and inauthentic – neither of which bodes well for your ability to positively influence others.

2. Be present.

Speak less and listen more to show that you're fully engaged in the present. It will tell you everything you need to know about a person's perspectives, desires, needs, and character. Active listening gives you an insight into people's emotional drives. Once you know the emotional drivers behind their thoughts and beliefs, you can

show them that you understand them.

If you're self-concerned, distracted, or seemingly insincere, you will lose the person from the onset, and they will be resistant to your influence despite efforts.

3. Ask questions.

Questions are more persuasive than other forms of verbal behavior. The more questions you ask, the more interested and engaged you appear. Therefore, the higher your chances of successfully influencing the person.

Asking open-ended questions is the key to learning about people's core values and drivers. Are they looking to gain admiration? Advance their careers? Make a difference in the world? Perhaps they are going through something in life.

Never forget that people do things for their own reasons; not yours. So, take as much time as needed to fully understand their deepest motivations. If you fail to influence someone, it's most likely because you don't know what was driving them.

4. Demonstrate authority

People are predisposed to listening to those with perceived authority. If you want influence and power, demonstrate authority in the area where you want to influence them. Experts always come with facts.

5. Acknowledge objections.

It's important that you never make people feel like they are wrong. If you do this, they will be triggered, and it'll be harder to steer them in the direction you want. Instead, acknowledge any objection they may have and address the suspicions. Doing that gives you credibility and allows you to proffer a solution.

6. Offer lavish but sincere praise.

Dale Carnegies emphasizes the essence of complimenting people you're trying to influence in his book, *How to Win Friends and Influence People*. Compliments and praises make people feel important and demonstrate your admiration of them, but only if you're earnest. Everyone wants sincere praise. But be careful of the thin line between praise and flattery.

7. Lead by example.

There's nothing more inspiring to people than seeing passion and talent at work. It's why people who aren't athletic in the least can be inspired by athletic prowess. Humans are wired to appreciate the extraordinary. You don't have to be extraordinary to influence people, but you certainly have to lead by example by demonstrating excellence.

Last Chance to Learn to Build a Tougher Mind

SCAN THE QR CODE NOW

CONCLUSION

You've made it to the end of this journey through the web of dark psychology – congratulations! In this book, we explored dark psychology and manipulation tactics used by those who seek to control and exploit others.

We delved into the realms of the Dark Triad traits, covert manipulation, gaslighting, and love bombing, putting the spotlight on strategies and methods deployed to deceive and subdue unsuspecting minds.

Yet, within the pages of this book, we've also explored a roadmap to help you fortify yourself against these insidious means of control. Knowledge is your greatest ally, and I hope you feel empowered to recognize warning signs and protect your emotional and mental well-being.

Armed with the knowledge in this book, you now know how to set healthy boundaries, build self-awareness, and nurture your assertiveness skills. You have learned the art of critical thinking and can question the narratives evil people present to you to unmask their hidden agendas by decoding body language clues.

As we conclude this book, remember that protecting yourself from dark psychology and manipulation is an ongoing process. It requires constant introspection, vigilance, and a commitment to growth.

Now, it's time to forge ahead, guided by this book and your unwavering spirit, as you navigate interpersonal interactions while preserving your independence and autonomy, and building meaningful connections.

Printed in Great Britain
by Amazon